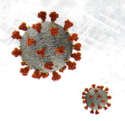

THE ECONOMIC IMPACT OF COVID-19

BY JILL C. WHEELER

CONTENT CONSULTANT
Tyler Schipper, PhD
Associate Professor
Department of Economics
University of St. Thomas

An Imprint of Abdo Publishing
abdobooks.com

ABDOBOOKS.COM

Published by Abdo Publishing, a division of ABDO, PO Box 398166, Minneapolis, Minnesota 55439. Copyright © 2023 by Abdo Consulting Group, Inc. International copyrights reserved in all countries. No part of this book may be reproduced in any form without written permission from the publisher. Essential Library™ is a trademark and logo of Abdo Publishing.

Printed in the United States of America, North Mankato, Minnesota.
052022
092022

Cover Photo: Spencer Platt/Getty Images News/Getty Images
Interior Photos: Lynne Sladky/AP Images, 4; Shutterstock Images, 8, 20, 53, 73, 80, 85; Jessica Christian/The San Francisco Chronicle/Hearst Newspapers/Getty Images, 11; National Photo Company Collection/Library of Congress, 14; China Topix/AP Images, 16; Charlie Neibergall/AP Images, 26; Red Line Editorial, 29; Damian Dovarganes/AP Images, 30; David Crigger/Bristol Herald Courier/AP Images, 32; Michael Siluk/Education Images/Universal Images Group/Getty Images, 38; STRF/Star Max/IPX/AP Images, 43, 89; David J. Phillip/AP Images, 46; Dmitry Kalinovsky/Shutterstock Images, 48; Michael Loccisano/Getty Images News/Getty Images, 51; Light Field Studios/Shutterstock Images, 55; Rich Graessle/Icon Sportswire/Getty Images, 60; Bing Guan/Bloomberg/Getty Images, 67; David Zalubowski/AP Images, 70; Prostock Studio/Shutterstock Images, 79; Elise Amendola/AP Images, 86; Victor Koldunov/Alamy, 90; Steven Senne/AP Images, 92; Georg Wendt/Picture Alliance/Getty Images, 98

Editor: Marie Pearson
Designer: Becky Daum

Library of Congress Control Number: 2021951389
Publisher's Cataloging-in-Publication Data
Names: Wheeler, Jill C., author.
Title: The economic impact of covid-19 / by Jill C. Wheeler
Description: Minneapolis, Minnesota : Abdo Publishing, 2023 | Series: Fighting covid-19 | Includes online resources and index.
Identifiers: ISBN 9781532197970 (lib. bdg.) | ISBN 9781098271626 (ebook)
Subjects: LCSH: COVID-19 (Disease)--Juvenile literature. | Economics--Juvenile literature. | Finance, Personal--Juvenile literature. | Unemployment--Social aspects--Juvenile literature. | Business losses--Juvenile literature. | Civilization, Modern--21st century--Juvenile literature. | United States--History--Juvenile literature.
Classification: DDC 614.592--dc23

CONTENTS

CHAPTER ONE
UNPRECEDENTED AID
4

CHAPTER TWO
COVID-19 RECESSION
16

CHAPTER THREE
LABOR IN THE SPOTLIGHT
26

CHAPTER FOUR
SHUTTERED DOORS
38

CHAPTER FIVE
BOOM TIMES
48

CHAPTER SIX
BREAKS IN THE CHAIN
60

CHAPTER SEVEN
EVERYONE HAS TO EAT
70

CHAPTER EIGHT
MOVING UP, MOVING OUT
80

CHAPTER NINE
HEALTH-CARE BILLS
90

ESSENTIAL FACTS	100	INDEX	110
GLOSSARY	102	ABOUT THE AUTHOR	112
ADDITIONAL RESOURCES	104	ABOUT THE CONSULTANT	112
SOURCE NOTES	106		

CHAPTER ONE

UNPRECEDENTED AID

The eyes of major corporations and small businesses alike were on the US Department of Labor on March 26, 2020. Department of Labor officials were set to release their weekly report on the number of Americans filing new claims for unemployment benefits. The Department of Labor reports are considered important indicators of economic activity, with the ability to influence stock markets depending on what they reveal. Stock markets reflect the activities of the buyers and sellers of stocks, which represent investments in companies.

The rapidly evolving global COVID-19 pandemic was shaking stock markets around the world. On February 19, the S&P 500, which tracks the performance of 500 large US corporations, had closed at a record high level. Less than ten days later, global stock markets

Some companies, including the hotel management company SBE, provided care packages to their furloughed employees in March 2020.

experienced their largest single-week decline since the 2008 global financial crisis.

    The March 26 unemployment report revealed that more American workers had filed for unemployment in the week ending March 21, 2020, than at any other time since modern figures began being tracked in 1967. According to Department of Labor figures, a record 3.28 million Americans had filed for unemployment, confirming what many economic analysts already suspected. Jerome Powell is the chair of the US Federal Reserve Board. This government agency manages the nation's money supply to support the economy and fight inflation. Inflation is an increase in the cost of goods and services. Powell stated, "We may well be in a recession."[1] A recession is a period of time when an economy gets smaller instead of larger.

    For many professionals who study labor markets, the numbers made sense. Growing concerns about COVID-19 had led to many lockdowns, which were restrictions on businesses and other activities. The goal of lockdowns was to slow the spread of disease. Yet the lockdowns also meant many people were unable to report to work, even if only for a short time. In this way, the spike in unemployment claims was unlike previous situations.

ENTER THE CARES ACT

The Department of Labor report added urgency to ongoing negotiations in the US Congress over a massive economic stabilization plan. Economic stabilization is when the government provides money to individuals and families or businesses so they can continue to buy goods and services that support other individuals, families, and businesses. Services are instances in which consumers pay others to provide a benefit. One day earlier, on March 25, the Senate with Senate Majority Leader Mitch McConnell had unanimously approved nearly $2 trillion for the plan.[2]

DEFINING A RECESSION

The official COVID-19 recession was short in comparison with previous recessions. Yet it still qualified as a recession according to the National Bureau of Economic Research (NBER). The NBER defines a recession as a significant decline in economic activity, which is seen in changes to employment, industrial production, how much people can purchase with their income, the gross domestic product (GDP), and wholesale and retail sales.

The COVID-19 recession was caused by the sudden economic shock that resulted from a virtual stop to some business activity. Past recessions had been caused by excessive debt, such as the Great Recession (2007–2009), and technological change, such as the upheaval created by the Industrial Revolution (1760–1840).

COVID-19 BY THE NUMBERS

VISUALIZING ONE TRILLION

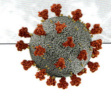

By 2021, Congress had passed various measures totaling to approximately $4 trillion to help address job loss and food insecurity, aid vaccine development and distribution, provide COVID-19 testing, help schools and businesses keep running, and assist state and local governments.[3] One trillion also can be thought of as one million million. It can be hard to visualize the scope of a number as large as one trillion. Consider a football field filled with one trillion $1 bills. It would take approximately 516,705 bills to cover the field in a single layer. If more layers of $1 bills were stacked up to equal $1 trillion, the stack would be 693 feet (211 m) tall.

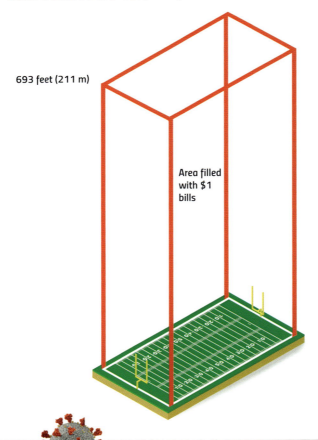

693 feet (211 m)

Area filled with $1 bills

On March 27, the House of Representatives with House Speaker Nancy Pelosi approved the legislation on a near-unanimous voice vote. President Donald Trump signed the measure into law within hours of House approval. The legislation became known as the Coronavirus Aid, Relief, and Economic Security (CARES) Act.

The CARES Act was the largest economic stimulus package in US history. The money provided for in the act was equal to 45 percent of all federal spending in 2019, the year before the COVID-19 pandemic began.[4] The expansive package included direct payments to individuals and married couples,

A TALE OF TWO STIMULUS PACKAGES

The CARES Act was just the first of several programs designed to ease the economic impact of COVID-19. Yet it was not the first time federal spending was used to boost an ailing economy. The Great Recession affected economies around the world. In response, the US government cut taxes, gave money to banks to keep them in business, and increased unemployment and food stamp benefits from 2008 to 2012. The COVID-19 stimulus packages through July 1, 2020, and the Great Recession stimulus packages were equal to roughly 2.3 and 2.4 percent, respectively, of national GDP at the time. This means the packages for both recessions were similar in size compared with the size of the economy. However, economic assistance for the Great Recession lasted roughly five years. The majority of COVID-19 aid was distributed in six months.[5]

additional unemployment benefits, and money to help businesses remain open. In addition, the CARES Act provided funds for health-care operations and covered the costs of COVID-19 testing and vaccination.

The act helped millions of Americans cover their bills. It provided direct payments of up to $1,200 for individuals and $2,400 for married couples, depending on household income. An additional $500 payment was included for each child in the household. Anyone who had filed a tax return qualified for these payments. While an estimated 160 million households had received their payments by the summer of 2020, another five to ten million households had not. Those households were more likely to be low-income households that typically did not file tax returns.

For those who had permanently or temporarily lost their jobs, the act extended the amount of time that people would receive unemployment benefits. For four months, it also added a $600 payment on top of the regular unemployment payments.[6] In addition, the act extended benefits to individuals who did not usually qualify for unemployment, including self-employed people and gig workers. Most gig workers are independent contractors who do short-term or project-based work for multiple clients.

A BOOST TO BUSINESS

Small businesses with fewer than 500 employees also received support, including loans so they could continue paying workers despite less business. In some cases, the

Small businesses, such as dance studios, lost revenue during lockdowns. Many needed the financial aid from the CARES Act to stay afloat.

> ### FIGHTING CARES FRAUD
>
> The CARES Act was intended to help vulnerable individuals and small businesses weather the worst of the coronavirus pandemic. The act involved a lot of money, which made it a target for people seeking to get those funds illegally. Within a year of passing the CARES Act, the US Department of Justice had charged nearly 500 people with fraud or other criminal schemes related to pandemic aid.[9] Activities ranged from fraudulent unemployment claims to creating fake companies to benefit from paycheck protection loans. The House's Select Subcommittee on the Coronavirus Crisis has indicated these initial charges were just the tip of the iceberg, and total fraudulent activity could ultimately amount to billions of dollars.

loans would be forgiven. Corporations with more than 500 employees likewise gained access to loans and other investments. Airlines in particular benefited from the CARES Act, with nearly $60 billion in assistance for passenger and cargo airlines alone.[7]

When the CARES Act passed, the United States had recorded the most COVID-19 cases in the world, with more than 92,000 cases and nearly 1,400 deaths.[8] Local, state, and federal authorities were struggling to contain the spread of the disease while reducing its economic impact. Many states had already announced stay-at-home orders, which severely restricted business activity for certain industries and led to the record-breaking unemployment filings in late March 2020.

By mid-July 2020, the National Bureau of Economic Research (NBER) reported that the COVID-19 recession was over. Lasting from just February to April, it was the shortest recession in US history. Even though economists had declared the recession over, millions of people still felt its impacts as the year went on. Gross domestic product (GDP) in the second quarter of 2020 had its biggest drop in history. GDP is the monetary value of all final goods and services produced within a nation's geographic borders over a specified period of time.

COVID-19 IN PERSPECTIVE

Throughout history, epidemics and pandemics have taken economic as well as human tolls. Depending on their length and severity, pandemics can reshape economies and create lasting impacts. For example, the 1918 influenza pandemic led people to save more of their money. It also led to fewer eligible workers searching for jobs.

Yet the COVID-19 pandemic was also unique compared to past pandemics. After World War II (1939–1945), the US government began using changes in federal spending and tax rates to increase economic activity, such as

Because the 1918 influenza pandemic killed many working-age people, a worker shortage resulted.

employment or sales, during times of economic stress. The CARES Act is an example of this practice, which is called fiscal policy. Likewise, social safety nets such as unemployment insurance are relatively new additions to the economic landscape. The option of working from home also is new within the modern economy and has played a significant role in the economic impact of

COVID-19. Finally, unlike with COVID-19, a vaccine was never developed during the 1918 pandemic.

The economic impact of COVID-19 is complex. It has changed how people feel about work and changed what it may take to get them back on the job. The pandemic has altered how people spend their time and their money. It has devastated some industries while minting new millionaires in others. It has called even more attention to the interconnected, global nature of the modern economy. The economic challenges of COVID-19 came not only because people got sick but also because of underlying factors and trends that were present long before COVID-19. As policymakers, elected leaders, and businesses continued working their way through the pandemic, they looked for potential solutions to address these underlying issues as well.

> "The coronavirus outbreak is economically akin to a major hurricane occurring in every state around the country for weeks on end."[10]
>
> —Daniel Zhao, economist, Glassdoor

CHAPTER TWO

COVID-19 RECESSION

The US economy was on solid ground on New Year's Eve in 2019, when news reports first mentioned an unusual new virus detected in Wuhan, China. The virus would later be called SARS-CoV-2. The disease it causes is COVID-19. At that time, the United States was enjoying an 11-year economic expansion, the longest in US history. That expansion, which came after the collapse of the US housing market in 2008, had delivered a long, gradual rise in GDP, with an average annual increase of 2.3 percent.[1] In 2019, the Dow Jones Industrial Average, an index that tracks the performance of 30 large, publicly owned companies, turned in its best performance since 2017. At the end of 2019, the S&P 500 was valued at 29 percent more than at the start of the year.[2]

    That situation began to change in late February 2020 as more and more reports of COVID-19 surfaced from

Places around the world, including Wuhan, China, suffered economically because of COVID-19 and the stay-at-home and quarantine orders that were intended to slow its spread.

> ## GDP
>
> GDP is calculated by taking the value of all the goods and services that have been produced within a country in a certain period minus the value of the goods and services that were needed to produce them. GDP gives information about the size of an economy and whether it is expanding or contracting. The US government began using GDP as a measure of economic health in 1991. The data gathered to create the measure turned out to be helpful in reducing the severity and duration of economic downturns. In 1999, the US Department of Commerce deemed GDP its "achievement of the century."[6]

around the world. Lab testing had confirmed the first US case of COVID-19 on January 20. By March 4, the United States was reporting more than 100 cases in a day.[3] Global stock markets reflected the anxiety of investors as consumers trimmed spending because of economic uncertainties or safety-based restrictions, and businesses responded by reducing operations or temporarily closing. The Dow plunged more than 2,000 points on March 9, losing more than 8 percent of its value. It was the worst one-day point decline in the Dow's history up to that point.[4] The following week, the US Department of Labor reported that 256,000 Americans had filed initial claims to collect unemployment benefits.[5] That would be the last week with fewer than 300,000 unemployment claims until October 2021.

By March 10, the United States had reported more than 1,000 COVID-19 cases. Layoffs and furloughs, or temporary layoffs, quickly followed as consumers began to stay home for fear of becoming infected, and businesses reduced costs as revenue shriveled. On March 11, the World Health Organization (WHO) declared the COVID-19 outbreak a pandemic. The next day, the Dow fell more than 2,300 points to close with a nearly 10 percent drop.[7]

Then, on March 16, the White House issued guidelines for the public, which included avoiding unnecessary travel, shopping trips, and social visits, as well as avoiding eating and drinking in bars, restaurants, and public food courts. The guidelines were intended to stretch the amount of time between new COVID-19 infections to buy

> ## EMPLOYMENT
>
> The US Department of Labor reports total nonfarm payroll employment numbers, including the number of people filing for unemployment, as one of the nation's primary economic indicators. The report is released on the first Friday of every month, making it one of the first clues analysts use in predicting what will happen in the economy. The report also details changes in the labor force participation rate. The labor force participation rate is the sum of all workers who are working or actively seeking a job divided by the total number of people who could be working. This number is important as it hints at the percentage of people who have become discouraged in their job search and are no longer actively looking for a job.

time to better respond to the virus. This idea was referred to as flattening the curve. The same day the guidelines were issued, the Dow lost nearly 3,000 points for a drop of almost 13 percent of its value.[8] That made March 16 an even worse day for the market than the October 28, 1929, stock market crash that ushered in the Great Depression (1929–1939).

PANIC AND SHUTDOWNS

Reaction to the guidelines and the stock market crash was swift. Many state, city, and business leaders quickly asked citizens and employees to stay home whenever possible.

Flattening the curve meant spreading out the number of infections over time so as to not overwhelm the health-care system.

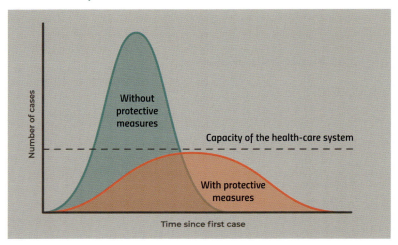

Other leaders passed new rules that required people to stay home with only a few exceptions. In-person events from business conferences to concerts and shows were postponed, canceled, or held virtually. Service businesses including movie theaters, gyms, and salons went dark. Airports and hotels emptied, and rental cars remained in their lots. Those employees who could work from home often did. Others found themselves out of a job or working significantly reduced hours.

Many retail and manufacturing businesses also announced they were temporarily closing their doors or suspending operations to slow the spread of the virus. Businesses deemed essential, including grocery stores, food processing operations, and health-care facilities, remained open. Those employees were asked to continue working as usual.

Around the country, the streets and sidewalks of urban centers rapidly emptied. In downtown Washington, DC, the daytime population dropped 82 percent between February 2020 and February 2021.[9] With few people commuting to DC offices, the businesses that normally served those workers found themselves with fewer customers than before. Within a matter of days, an

> "If I don't open, I don't sell, and that means no money. It's that simple. It's terrifying."[11]
>
> —Illyne Ganley, owner of the Beauty Lounge in Summit, New Jersey

expanding economy had become a shrinking one.

The CARES Act reassured the markets. By April 7, the stock market had largely stabilized, even though it would not reach its pre-pandemic levels again until November. The work ahead in rebuilding the larger economy, however, had only just begun.

LAYOFFS AND FURLOUGHS

A CNBC/SurveyMonkey poll of small business owners in late April 2020 put numbers to the economic impact Americans were witnessing. Twenty-nine percent of respondents to the survey indicated they had been forced to close their in-person operations, and 25 percent had closed their entire businesses temporarily. Thirty-six percent of small business owners surveyed said they had cut their own pay, and 15 percent reported they had furloughed some or all of their employees. Another 14 percent had laid off some or all of their employees.[10]

As businesses laid off or furloughed more employees, worker safety nets began to fray. Unemployment websites in Kentucky, Oregon, and New York were among the systems that crashed the week of March 16 due to the heavy increase in activity. By April, the US unemployment rate had reached 14.8 percent, the highest rate recorded since data collection began in 1948.[12]

Many of the workers who remained had their hours reduced. The average number of weekly hours worked in production and manufacturing—a key indicator of the economy's health—dropped from 41.6 hours on average in February 2020 to 38.4 hours in April.[13] Jobs in these industries include work at car factories and meat processing plants.

PRICES AND PURCHASES

Businesses cut costs in other areas too. Some reduced or stopped contributing to employee retirement plans. Firms also benefited from a dramatic drop in business travel expenses. A survey of US-based companies found that most experienced a 90 percent or higher drop in business travel expenses in early 2020.[14]

The pandemic also led to changes in how consumers shopped. Retail sales in April 2020 fell but eventually recovered. Much of the sales activity switched to online retailers, with online sales growing significantly in the second quarter of 2020 as more people shopped from their homes. Even as consumers showed their willingness to shop online, they continued to show concern about what was to come. The Consumer Confidence Index uses monthly surveys to gauge how optimistic consumers are about the future of the economy. Survey responses are used to create an index where values above 100 indicate consumers are optimistic, and values below 100 indicate they are more pessimistic. The index had reached a near-historic high of 106 early in the first quarter of 2020 but then dropped to 92 in the second quarter.[15] Routine surveys of global consumer confidence found that consumers were far less optimistic about the future in the second quarter of 2020 than they had been at the end of 2019. With job prospects slipping and anxiety rising, millions of consumers cut back on spending on non-essentials. At the same time, COVID-19 restrictions further limited sales in categories such as eating out, entertainment, and clothing for work.

In September 2020, the US Department of Commerce released official numbers for the GDP in the second quarter of 2020. While the department previously had reported a 5 percent decline in GDP for the first quarter of 2020, the number for the second quarter was staggering. For the period from April to June, GDP dropped at an annualized rate of more than 31 percent, the largest drop in US history.[16] This means that if the reduction in economic activity from April to June 2020 had lasted for a full year, the US economy would have shrunk by one-third over the course of that year.

> **CONSUMER CONFIDENCE**
>
> If consumers are confident that they will continue to have money to spend, they are more likely to buy goods and services. So consumer confidence matters because much economic activity in most countries is due to people buying goods and services. Consumer confidence in the United States is measured by a monthly survey of 5,000 households to inform the Consumer Confidence Index. The survey is conducted by an independent research association called the Conference Board. The federal government, businesses, and investors use the index, along with other tools, to predict how likely consumers are to keep spending money.

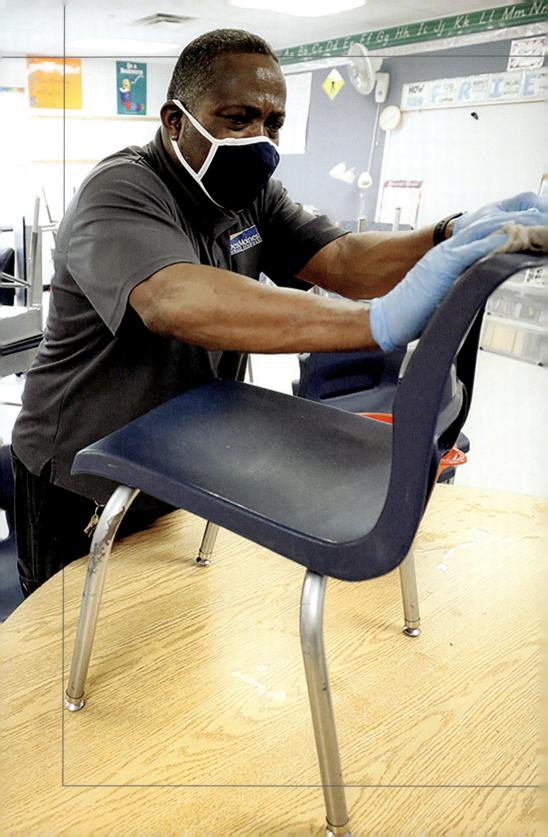

CHAPTER THREE

LABOR IN THE SPOTLIGHT

Few areas of the economy suffered a greater impact from the COVID-19 pandemic than labor markets. The COVID-19 pandemic created three different groups of workers: those who could safely work from home, those who had to show up for their jobs despite health threats, and those who lost their jobs as a result of the recession. In April 2020 alone, the COVID-19 pandemic led to the loss of some 20.5 million jobs.[1] The pre-pandemic February 2020 unemployment rate was just 3.5 percent.[2]

These job losses, however, did not occur equally across worker demographics. Job losses tied to COVID-19 were greater for women, workers of color, workers in low-wage jobs, and workers with less education. Younger workers also experienced higher rates of unemployment. In this sense, the pandemic amplified

Many people, such as custodians, did not have the option to work from home during the pandemic. These people faced a higher risk of exposure to COVID-19.

WHEN ECONOMIES BECOME SICK

COVID-19 is not the first disease to sicken both humans and an economy. During the Black Death (1348–1351), the bubonic plague killed 60 million people, primarily people in poverty suffering from malnutrition. These people also made up much of the workforce. The post-pandemic worker shortage in England led to an increase in wages as employers picked from a smaller pool of remaining workers.

existing inequalities in the workplace, as unemployment rates for Black and Latino workers have been consistently higher than those of white workers.

A HIGHER TOLL

By the end of 2020, even after some jobs were recovered, women had lost a net of 5.4 million jobs during the pandemic, which was nearly one million more jobs lost than men.[3] Black and Latino workers likewise reported higher unemployment rates than white workers. The September 2020 unemployment rates for Black and Latino workers were 11.5 percent and 10 percent, respectively, compared with 6.8 percent for white workers.[4] These higher rates were partly due to the tendency for these groups to be overrepresented in businesses that depend on delivering in-person services, which were the businesses most affected by the pandemic.

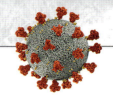

COVID-19 BY THE NUMBERS

WORKFORCE EARLY UNEMPLOYMENT RATES[5]

Spikes in unemployment caused by the COVID-19 pandemic captured headlines in March and April 2020. Yet many analysts said the way the government typically measures unemployment failed to reflect the full economic pain of the pandemic. The measures did not capture workers whose hours were reduced but who still had jobs, for example. The numbers also failed to reflect people who wanted to work but stopped searching for jobs because none were available in their industry. Finally, conventional measures cannot differentiate between people who were temporarily laid off versus those who were permanently laid off. When all of these situations are factored in, researchers can estimate the percentage of the US workforce that experienced a layoff or reduction in hours because of COVID-19.

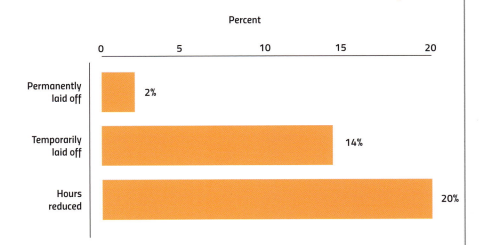

Early in the pandemic, there were not enough jobs available for those who wanted to work.

Wage rates also played a role in determining which jobs were lost. Some 56 percent of the jobs lost between February 2020 and September 2021 were in the lowest-paying industries. However, these industries represent just 30 percent of all jobs, meaning they were hit especially hard.[6] Low-paying industries include leisure and hospitality businesses such as restaurants, hotels, events, entertainment venues, and transportation.

These also were industries with a high level of in-person service, so they had a higher risk of disease transmission.

Worker education levels also were reflected in pandemic unemployment numbers. Between January 2020 and July 2021, workers with less than a high school diploma faced a peak unemployment rate of 21 percent. This was in contrast to a peak unemployment rate of 8.4 percent for workers who had a bachelor's degree or higher. In addition, workers ages 20 to 24 had greater peak unemployment rates than those ages 25 to 54. The younger workers' peak rate was more than 23 percent, while the older workers' was under 14 percent.[7]

ROBOTS DON'T GET SICK

The COVID-19 pandemic has accelerated an existing trend of replacing low-wage workers with technology, including robots. Unlike humans, robots do not get sick, do not need any bathroom breaks, and can work around the clock. Early in the pandemic, some businesses began using robots to clean floors, deliver room service in hotels, and guard empty buildings, among other jobs. Chatbots, which are computer programs designed to simulate conversation with human users, also saw a bump as the pandemic sent call center workers home. Software company LivePerson reported a fourfold increase in its business in March 2020. The company says its software enables companies to turn 1,000-person call centers into 100-person call centers by using its chatbots.

In addition to a greater risk of sickness, frontline workers often faced overwhelming workloads.

ON THE FRONT LINES

For those workers who did not lose their jobs or could not work from home, the COVID-19 pandemic still presented significant challenges. Workers in essential jobs—which included grocery store and drugstore workers, public transit drivers, truckers, janitorial workers, postal workers, warehouse workers, and health-care, childcare, and social service workers—were expected to show up each day healthy and ready to work. Women and workers of color were overrepresented in these fields.[8]

Many of these frontline jobs did not include health insurance or paid sick time. Workers exposed to COVID-19 on the job who became sick faced lost wages as well as disease symptoms, the potential to infect other family members, and medical bills. To address this, Congress passed the Families First Coronavirus Response Act in March 2020 to help provide for paid sick leave. Because of exemptions for the largest and the smallest employers, only about 12 percent of workers who likely had to continue working during the pandemic were qualified for the program.[9]

In addition, many frontline workers did not have access to childcare when schools closed because of COVID-19. This situation was especially problematic for women of color. Mothers of color are more likely to be single and therefore the primary source of income for their households. These women faced additional childcare costs for an unknown period of time so they

HELP FOR GIG WORKERS

From entertainers to fitness instructors to housekeepers, millions of gig workers were out of work because of the pandemic. Many got help from the Pandemic Unemployment Assistance (PUA) program. The PUA, part of the CARES Act, was the first federal program designed to help independent workers, who do not usually qualify for unemployment benefits.

Millions of gig workers received PUA benefits in the summer of 2020. The program was phased out in 2021. Advocates for independent contractors say the strong interest in the PUA program shows the importance of making unemployment benefits available to gig workers as well as traditional workers.

could continue working. Big differences in unemployment rates, wages, and benefits between female and male workers and between workers of color and white workers became even more pronounced. These differences continued to affect the labor market even as the disease threat changed over time.

A CHANGING WORKFORCE

The pandemic accelerated workplace trends that had already started. Many low-wage industries such as trucking and home health assistance had worker shortages even before the pandemic. Job losses and working conditions in these sectors became even more pronounced during the pandemic. As a result, the workers who remained willing to take these jobs could demand higher wages. Workers without college degrees began calling for more money than before the pandemic to take such jobs, which typically require them to work on-site.

Even after the arrival of COVID-19 vaccines in December 2020, many businesses struggled to fill low-wage jobs. By December, US employers reported 10.9 million job openings, while just 6.3 million workers were classified as unemployed.[10] The continued spread of COVID-19 in 2021 discouraged many people from taking jobs that involved ongoing exposure to the virus. Uncertain childcare situations created challenges for other employees. They may have lost access to the childcare providers they used before, and they were uncertain if schools would once again shift to remote learning.

> "Let's face it, even $20 per hour with few if any benefits isn't a princely sum."[11]
>
> —Joshua Shapiro, chief US economist, Maria Fiorini Ramirez Inc. consultancy

These concerns led to an increase in average hourly wages in those industries most desperate to hire workers, including at restaurants, bars, and hotels. Labor market analysts expected this trend to continue as more workers entered the labor market with more education and fewer employees sought out blue-collar or service jobs. This meant industries that historically employed workers with less than a college degree would have a harder time filling those jobs well into the future and would need to pay higher wages to do so.

REMOTE WORK GROWS

The pandemic caused an increase in remote work options. Before COVID-19, only about 6 percent of workers worked mainly from home. By May 2020, more than one-third of employees worked from home. Compared to people with lower levels of education, people with bachelor's degrees or higher were more

MORE DIGITAL NOMADS

The rise of technologies including the internet, mobile phones, and videoconferencing let more people continue working even as they travel around the world. In 2019, seven million Americans were digital nomads. In 2020, that number shot up to nearly 11 million.[12] This shift was driven in part by traditional workers who suddenly found themselves working remotely. Many used this unique situation to explore working from one or more new locations. The trend also was a bonus for home-sharing sites such as Airbnb and Vrbo. Airbnb reported that the number of long stays, lasting four or more weeks, nearly doubled between 2019 and the beginning of 2021.[13]

likely to work from home. In some industries, roughly three-quarters of the employee base could work from home early in the pandemic.[14] These industries included office-based businesses and professional occupations such as engineering, legal, and education jobs.

Fears of infection in the workplace lingered, and many saw the benefits of working from home. Many employees preferred full-time work-from-home arrangements or a permanent hybrid model, with some time at the office and some time at home. A July 2021 survey found that most people who were working from home would accept a pay cut of up to 5 percent so they could continue working from home.[15]

CHAPTER FOUR

SHUTTERED DOORS

The COVID-19 pandemic shifted how Americans spent their money. While lockdowns and stay-at-home orders initially reduced sales of both goods and services, the pandemic affected service businesses harder in the long term. In 2019, about 64 percent of Americans' spending went toward services. Between February and April 2020, consumers reduced their spending on services by 20 percent.[1] Spending on services began to climb again after April. But by the end of 2020, it still had not reached pre-pandemic levels.

Fears of the virus meant the hardest-hit service businesses were those that involved consumers sharing space with people outside their immediate households. Airports, hotels, gyms, restaurants, bars, sporting events, concerts, and conferences all fell into this category. A few services, however, thrived during the pandemic. These included food delivery services

Instead of buying services, many people purchased more goods and had them delivered to their homes.

and home service calls. In June 2021, home service calls rose dramatically as consumers sought out contractors for home remodeling projects. Reduced spending on some services, along with receiving stimulus payments, made more money available for these services that did not require as much person-to-person contact.

WORKOUTS

COVID-19 created significant changes in how people approached exercise and fitness. With many gyms and fitness studios closed, consumers found other ways to work out, both outside and inside their homes. Some fitness businesses offered temporary solutions, including personal outdoor domes with speakers for class instruction. Others turned their parking lots into socially distanced classrooms. Yet for many consumers, there was no going back. A July 2020 survey found that 24 percent of people who regularly went to a gym before COVID-19 were unlikely to return to a shared gym.[2] Many of the respondents said they preferred the convenience and flexibility of working out at home and felt they were in better shape than before the pandemic.

THE BIGGEST LOSERS

As lockdowns changed personal travel plans and teleconferences replaced in-person meetings, the travel and hospitality industries shrank rapidly. Between February and May 2020, rail and air travel plummeted by 96 and 91 percent, respectively. Before COVID-19, the airline industry had been experiencing record success.[3] By September 2020, passenger numbers had dropped to just 27.1 million. That was 59 million fewer passengers than in September 2019.[4] Even driving trips dropped at this time, though not as drastically because car trips were sometimes substituted for rail and air travel. Hotels felt the loss. The American Hotel and Lodging Association, a trade association that represents the hotel industry, reported its membership lost more than 4.8 million hospitality and leisure jobs and more than $45 billion in room revenue because of the pandemic.[5]

Restaurants were another industry hit hard. The National Restaurant Association (NRA) reported that the restaurant industry

TICKET TO STREAM

The sudden halt in most live performances created challenges for performers who depended on ticket sales and tips to make a living. As fans retreated to their living rooms, artists found new ways to meet them there. Headliners including Niall Horan, Billie Eilish, Keith Urban, and John Legend streamed intimate concerts on platforms including Twitch, Instagram, and subscription streaming services. Many other musicians and artists, from comedians to drag performers, also moved their acts to virtual platforms and collected tips that way too. Fans could support their favorite artists during livestreams by sending money through apps such as Venmo, Cash App, and PayPal.

> **HIGHER EDUCATION**
>
> US colleges and universities suffered heavy financial losses from the COVID-19 pandemic. As cases mounted in the spring of 2020, most colleges closed dormitories and sent students home to avoid spreading infections. Many students, meanwhile, decided they did not want to pay tuition for remote learning and either took time off or avoided re-enrolling. Freshman enrollment dropped 13 percent overall as a result of the pandemic, with community colleges facing a nearly 19 percent drop in new students.[8]

lost $130 billion in sales between February and November 2020. An NRA survey of members indicated that 17 percent of restaurants closed for good during the pandemic, while 87 percent of restaurants still operating reported an average drop in sales revenue of 36 percent.[6] In comparison, an average of 5 percent of leisure and hospitality businesses, the category that includes restaurants, closed each year between 2009 and 2015.[7]

The cruise industry is among the highest-profile victims of the COVID-19 pandemic. COVID-19 outbreaks on cruise ships early in the pandemic led the US Centers for Disease Control and Prevention (CDC) to stop cruise ship operations at US ports in March 2020. According to the Cruise Lines International Association, the order

Many restaurants sat empty while lockdowns prevented people from dining in.

led to losses of $32 billion in 2020.[9] That figure includes the losses incurred by the other industries that support cruises, such as travel agencies and food and beverage suppliers. With no current revenues and no guarantee of when they could resume operations, some cruise companies took dramatic steps. Carnival Corporation, the world's largest cruise operator, accelerated plans to sell some of its less efficient ships.

43

Like the cruise industry, the rental car industry faced a sudden drop in bookings as Americans traveled less. Major rental car companies quickly sold off large parts of their fleets. The smaller fleets meant rental car companies lost less money in the early days of the pandemic. Yet after initial lockdowns ended, companies were unable to respond to a swift increase in demand as Americans chose cars over other forms of transit. Plus, companies couldn't quickly return to pre-pandemic operations because of labor shortages and a shortage of new vehicles to purchase. For consumers, it meant a rental car that cost $35 per day in 2019 was renting for nearly $99 per day in 2021.[10]

In addition to fewer sales, some of the hardest-hit industries also earned less money from each sale. Hotels and airlines slashed their prices in an effort to book rooms and seats. In 2020, the average cost of a domestic airline ticket was $292. That was the lowest average inflation-adjusted annual fare since the US Bureau of Transportation began collecting the information in 1995. In 2019, the average airfare had been $359.[11]

SMALL BUSINESSES HARMED

The majority of air travel, hotel stays, car rentals, and cruise purchases are booked through large publicly held corporations. Yet the US economy also includes millions of small businesses with significantly fewer resources. These businesses, defined as businesses with fewer than 500 employees, employ nearly half of American workers.

A survey of small business owners in the early days of the pandemic found that three-fourths had only enough cash on hand to last two months or less. More than 40 percent of the businesses surveyed said they already had temporarily closed, primarily because of the pandemic. Businesses operating in the food service, arts and entertainment, personal services, retail, and hospitality industries reported that they had reduced their

> "The normalcy we called pre-COVID, that no longer exists. We have to be prepared, on our toes, to adapt."[12]
>
> —Lyle Richardson, chief operating officer of A. Marshall Hospitality

Because small businesses often don't have a lot of money in savings, many small business owners worried that they did not have enough to make it through a lockdown.

employee base by 50 percent.[13] Businesses in the finance, real-estate, and professional services industries, such as law and accounting firms, experienced less disruption because they could shift to remote work.

Businesses in the retail sector, particularly those that did not have an online presence, were hit especially hard. In April 2020, retail sales fell 14.3 percent from the previous month. They later rebounded, helped largely by online sales. By July 2020, retail sales were up by 2.7 percent from February. Not all retailers shared the rebound. Sales at stores selling clothing and accessories were still nearly 20 percent lower in July 2020 than they had been that February.[14] Stores in central business districts that typically served commuters or that relied on foot traffic saw their sales plummet as well.

One silver lining to the COVID-19 pandemic was a significant increase in personal savings as many people reduced spending and received government stimulus checks. The personal savings rate, defined as the ratio of personal saving to disposable personal income, spiked. While saving money does not provide an immediate boost to the economy, some economists believe having more of a cash cushion can help households avoid taking out potentially risky loans in the future.

> ## THE HOTTEST ITEMS
> What people purchased during the COVID-19 pandemic offered a window into how the disease had altered daily life. The Willy Street Co-op in Madison, Wisconsin, shared a list in May 2020 of its most and least popular items based on sales. In addition to toilet paper and cleaning supplies, plenty of buyers wanted coffee filters, soy sauce, and sports drinks. The least popular items reflected a time when consumers sought fewer shopping trips, bought more food when they did shop, and had little opportunity to dress up and socialize. Unpopular items included fresh fruits and vegetables, nutrition bars, single-serving items, and personal care products such as cosmetics, hair styling gel, and breath mints.

CHAPTER FIVE

BOOM TIMES

A pandemic that discouraged face-to-face interaction was a benefit for those industries created to help people avoid such things. Big winners in the COVID-19 economy included businesses that made it possible to shop from home, work remotely, or fix up the homes and apartments where people were now spending most of their time. In addition, fears of catching COVID-19 led to increases in specific products and services aimed at avoiding infection. While demand for services overall was down, some services, such as cleaning or delivery services, experienced a boom in business. Products promoted as tools in the fight against COVID-19 also fared well, even if the data indicated they were less than effective.

The COVID-19 pandemic also turned into a win for investors. Following record losses, the stock market recovered in the second half of 2020. The Dow hit

Home repair and renovation workers were in high demand as people spent more time at home and less money on other services.

a record high on December 4, 2020, and the S&P 500 reached a new record on December 17, 2020. Thanks to actions by Congress and the Federal Reserve, companies could borrow money inexpensively to expand or keep going, and consumers still had money to spend. While this record performance was a bonus for individuals with money to invest, it also highlighted the disparities between those hardest hit by the pandemic and those who experienced little disruption.

ONLINE PURCHASES

In 2019, online sales accounted for less than 16 percent of US retail sales. In 2020, they accounted for nearly 20 percent of all sales.[1] Sometimes people shopped online because they were concerned about the safety of in-person shopping. Other times, especially at the very beginning of the pandemic, online sales helped some merchants continue making money after they had shut their doors to foot traffic.

Historically, most people had not purchased food online. The pandemic shifted that, with online purchases of food and drinks showing the greatest increase in online sales of any category between March 2020 and the end of the year. App-based grocery delivery service Instacart saw a massive increase. Founded in 2012 by Apoorva Mehta, the app had struggled over the years to become profitable. Instacart lost $300 million in 2019. By the end of April 2020, Instacart sales were up 450 percent from December 2019, and Mehta had become a billionaire.[2]

Through Instacart, people could select items they wanted to buy and enter payment information. An Instacart shopper would go to the store, purchase the items, and deliver them.

Both Amazon and Walmart also saw significant increases in their online grocery orders as well as increases in other categories. The pandemic, with its lockdowns and stay-at-home orders, also led some consumers to seek out at-home entertainment. Sales of books, musical instruments, and sporting goods likewise increased during the pandemic.

Still, an online presence was not a guarantee of sales success during COVID-19. Retailer JCPenney offered online as well as in-store purchases, yet the company filed for bankruptcy in May 2020. The company was among a number of large retailers that had been struggling prior to the pandemic. The retail upheavals caused by the COVID-19 pandemic simply sped up the process.

THE NBA'S BUBBLE

COVID-19 was a money loser for all professional sports, but the National Basketball Association (NBA) did better than others. The league consulted with scientists before developing what it called a bubble system, in which 22 teams all journeyed to Orlando, Florida, to play the final games of the 2019–2020 season at Walt Disney World Resort. All players stayed in one of three hotels, and no one was allowed inside the bubble without submitting two negative COVID-19 tests. The precautions and creativity that enabled the NBA to finish out its season meant the league lost $1.5 billion in 2020 compared with the NFL's $2 billion hit.[3]

Some people purchased more technology so they could play video games with friends online.

GAME ON

Another big winner during COVID-19 was the gaming industry. One survey found that 55 percent of people said they turned to video games to fill their time during the pandemic.[4] Many looked to multiplayer games to connect virtually. Microsoft reported a 130 percent increase in multiplayer engagement in March and April 2020, and it reported it reached a total of ten million users with a paid Game Pass subscription. Nintendo also cashed in during the pandemic, selling more than 13 million copies of *Animal Crossing: New Horizons*, a game released in late March 2020. Video game streaming platform Twitch, which is owned by Amazon, recorded a 50 percent increase in gaming hours watched from March to April of 2020.[5]

Video streaming services also gave people something to do at home. An October 2020 survey of 1,100 US consumers found that people paid for an average of five streaming-service subscriptions, up from three before COVID-19. Another survey found that 36 percent of consumers who increased their number of subscriptions during COVID said they would not have done so were it not for the pandemic.[6]

> "People are at home, they have nothing to do, they are not commuting. You have more time and you're bored."[7]
>
> —Michael Pachter, Wedbush Securities, on why gaming took off during the pandemic

HOME OFFICE OUTFITTERS

At the height of pandemic-related closures, many people worked from home. That created a scramble for the tools and technologies that allow people to collaborate remotely. Videoconferencing company Zoom made more money in the three months from May to July 2020

Desks, chairs, and various computer apps all saw increases in sales as more people began working from home.

than it had earned in all of 2019. The brand name Zoom even began to be used as a verb for video calls, as in "I will zoom you." While Zoom was becoming the common name for an entire category of videoconferencing options, other videoconferencing platforms were likewise growing. Microsoft reported that active users of its Teams videoconferencing platform grew from 32 million to 44 million in just one week in March 2020.[8] The Microsoft Azure cloud computing platform, as well as Alphabet's

WORK-FROM-HOME AND PRODUCTIVITY

For some Americans, COVID-19 removed their daily office commute and replaced it with a daily stream of videoconferences with the coworkers they used to see face-to-face. As businesses evaluated whether to bring employees back to the office, some wondered how work-from-home arrangements had affected productivity.

A small team of researchers tracked more than 30,000 workers beginning in May 2020. When they analyzed their data in March 2021, they found nearly six out of ten of the workers reported that they were more productive working from home than they had anticipated. Only 15 percent of the workers surveyed said they felt they were less productive at home than at the office. The research team estimated overall worker productivity could increase by 5 percent compared with pre-pandemic levels if remote workers continued working from home even after the pandemic ended.[9]

Google cloud computing platform, saw gains as well when more business and entertainment shifted online.

In addition to technology, the remote work situation created opportunities for companies making office furniture, computers, and webcams. In 2021, manufacturers of personal computers had their best year of sales since 2015, building on a boom in business that began during the pandemic.

While traditional office furniture manufacturers serving customers who need large-scale, professionally installed and designed workspaces saw their sales plummet, online furniture retailer Wayfair experienced significant growth as people outfitted their new home offices. The online furniture and home fashions retailer reported its first-ever profit in the second quarter of 2020.

SERVICE WINNERS

Despite downward pressure on service sales during COVID-19, some services thrived. Cleaning and delivery services were among the first to see a growth in demand. Leading that demand was an increased need for cleaning services in medical facilities and commercial businesses, such as restaurants. Delivery services also saw a spike in demand as people shied away from leaving their homes. These services stepped in to deliver supplies for businesses as well as consumer orders of food and other retail purchases.

People spending more time at home led to an increase in demand for landscaping and yard-care services. Tutors experienced a jump in business as parents sought extra help for their children when schools moved to online learning. Finally, both online behavioral health services and in-home health services faced an increase in demand as consumers sought help addressing the mental and physical health challenges of the pandemic.

PROFITS AND LOSSES

Other companies found alternate revenue streams during the pandemic by focusing on the market for personal health and safety. By early April, the chief executive officer of online marketplace Etsy said some 20,000 sellers on the platform were selling face masks.[10] While this product helped make up for lost sales of other products, some of the shopkeepers ended up with masks they could not sell as the introduction of COVID-19 vaccines began to reduce mask wearing.

The vaccines themselves created windfalls for several companies. The Moderna COVID-19 vaccine was the first-ever commercial product for the company, which had never made a profit before 2021. The company's 2021 sales topped $18 billion.[11]

CHINA CASHES IN

China was the only major global economy to grow in the initial pandemic year of 2020, recording 2.2 percent growth. In comparison, China's average annual growth rate was nearly 6 percent in 2019.[12] By the first quarter of 2021, it had roared back to record an 18.3 percent rise in GDP compared with the first quarter of 2020.[13] Analysts credit China's initial record-breaking growth, along with surging demand for electronics, to its early ability to contain the SARS-CoV-2 virus.

Pfizer, the manufacturer of another vaccine, reported that its vaccine brought in $3.5 billion in revenue in the first three months of 2021 alone.[14] Additionally, companies making air purifiers saw a 57 percent jump in business in 2020 as people purchased them to reduce the chances of getting infected.[15]

Early in the pandemic, a few small distilling businesses shifted from making products such as vodka, gin, and rum to making alcohol-based hand sanitizer. At that time, hand sanitizer was difficult to find and very expensive when it was available. The shift ended up costing some businesses a lot of money in lost sales with hand sanitizer they could not sell once major manufacturers caught up with demand.

LUXURY SANITIZER

Luxury French perfume brand LVMH was one of many companies that answered the call to pitch in during the COVID-19 pandemic. The company best known for its Christian Dior, Givenchy, and Guerlain brands quickly repurposed its factories to produce hand sanitizer for French hospitals. Within 72 hours, the company took the same purified water, ethanol, and glycerin it had on hand for perfume and made sanitizing gel instead. For the new product, it used machinery, plastic bottles, and pump dispensers that normally filled and held liquid soaps and moisturizers.

CHAPTER SIX

BREAKS IN THE CHAIN

US consumers were on edge in early March 2020 as global COVID-19 cases rose. Consumers began stocking up on supplies. This led to panic buying, which happens when people see other people buying something and they think they need to buy it too. Panic buying increased demand for toilet paper. In addition, people working from home needed more toilet paper, and product that was intended for businesses could not be readily moved to retail stores. Toilet paper sales on March 12, 2020, were up 734 percent from the same day one year earlier, and at grocery stores it became the top-selling product by dollars spent. By March 23, 70 percent of US grocery stores reported that they had no toilet paper to sell.[1]

    Toilet paper was among the first items to run out as the pandemic swept the world. Demand for hand sanitizer, surgical masks, respirators, disinfecting wipes,

Products such as food were sometimes sold out at stores as demand rose during the pandemic.

and other cleaning supplies also exceeded supply. In some cases, this led to price gouging, which is when sellers charge more than usual for high-demand products. Amazon fined several sellers for price gouging hand sanitizer, including a situation in which a bottle that normally cost from $21 to $35 was sold for more than $80.[2] As the pandemic wore on, consumers scrambled to find dumbbells, seeds, breakfast cereal, work-from-home desks, outdoor recreational equipment, and bleach as the pandemic changed lifestyles and habits almost overnight.

While unusual spikes in consumer demand caused the initial shortage, the resulting lag in supply uncovered difficult truths about the state of modern supply chains. Supply chains are defined as all the activities that go into producing and delivering a particular product to a consumer. Over the years, companies have worked to make their supply chains as efficient as possible. Large inventories of products waiting to be sold are a drag on profits, so companies keep less inventory. This strategy is called "just in time." It means products are manufactured and distributed right before they are needed. When demand skyrocketed, such as for toilet paper, there was no excess inventory to meet that demand. Once the available supply was sold, consumers had no choice but to wait until more could be manufactured. At the same time, these situations led to higher costs for businesses, which began passing these costs on to consumers. In April 2021, American consumers were paying 4.2 percent more on average for goods and services such as food, energy, and shelter than they had been a year prior, the largest 12-month increase since 2008.[3]

Then, as COVID-19 infections and illness spread, many factories shut down or reduced their hours of operation because workers were sick or were under stay-at-home orders. This further reduced the output of consumer goods. Many shipping firms responded to these reductions by trimming their schedules too.

JUST-IN-TIME MANUFACTURING

Just-in-time (JIT) manufacturing is a method of running a manufacturing company, which is a business that makes products. JIT focuses on finding the most efficient way to produce and distribute things. JIT manufacturing has been successful in helping companies improve their profits by reducing the amount of waste in their operations. Continuous improvement is a key element in JIT. This involves bringing together employees from different departments to work together on solving problems. In some cases, it has even improved how employees feel about their company.

Americans took the money they were saving on services and began to spend it on products. But increasing production was not as simple as keeping workers healthy. Modern supply chains rely on a web of interconnected companies producing the many parts that can go into a single product. A computer assembled in China might need a chip from Taiwan, a flat-screen display from South Korea, and specialty chemicals from Europe. Even if the Chinese computer factory was up and running normally, there was no guarantee that the factory could acquire everything it needed to make the computer.

CHIP SHORTAGE

Computer chips are key components in everything from cars and trucks to mobile phones, laptops, and gaming consoles. As the pandemic sent people away from schools and offices, there was a sudden increase in demand for computers and smartphones at home. Demand also jumped for game consoles. Companies making these products quickly ordered as many chips as they could get.

Automakers found themselves in a different situation. Modern cars can contain more than 3,000 chips each, though the total use of chips by the auto industry accounts for only about 3 percent of all chips sold.[4] As the pandemic cooled demand for new cars and trucks, the auto industry ordered fewer of them. Yet it wasn't long before demand returned. By this time, chips were in short supply.

With few to no chips, many auto manufacturers could not produce many vehicles, if any. In February 2021, General Motors closed a production plant in Kansas City, Missouri, because it had no chips. Mercedes-Benz chose to save the few chips it had for its higher-priced models, leaving consumers with fewer choices for cheaper alternatives. Combined with other supply chain challenges, the chip shortage led to a drop in vehicle production. Without many new cars to sell, auto

A PERFECT STORM

Not all supply challenges during the pandemic were caused by the pandemic itself. A record-breaking winter storm during February 2021 in the southern United States temporarily shut down three chip factories and five factories that produce a key chemical needed to make foam. The storm compounded the existing chip shortage, as well as a foam shortage created by high pandemic-induced demand for recreational vehicles, refrigerators, and furniture. In another case, an August 2020 fire at a chlorine manufacturing plant in Louisiana reduced chlorine production just as the pandemic had created increased demand for backyard swimming pools.

dealerships had empty lots. And prices for used cars were up 40 percent from their pre-pandemic levels.[5]

SHIPPING BOTTLENECKS

The pandemic also led to disruptions in how goods were delivered to stores and consumers. In turn, there were higher costs and delays for deliveries. In the early days of the pandemic, companies hustled to deliver pandemic supplies such as masks to ports around the world. Some of these ports, such as those in Africa and South America, were less profitable for shippers. The containers that held the masks were left there, empty, once the cargo was unloaded. Shipping companies focused their

DOLLAR STORE DOWN

Dollar stores sell many items for a dollar or less. In 2021, dollar stores made up nearly one-third of all stores announcing new locations. The stores had found success moving into inner cities and rural areas where other retailers were unwilling to make investments. That changed with COVID-19. The dollar store business model relied on low wages for its employees and a steady flow of inexpensive imported merchandise. But dollar stores faced significant challenges as the labor pool shriveled and supply chain hitches delayed merchandise shipments. The dollar store chain Dollar Tree said it expected that its freight costs alone would be an additional $200 million in 2021.[6]

Shipping ports filled up with containers during the pandemic.

efforts—and directed their shipping containers—to more profitable ports in Europe, North America, and Asia.

As American consumers began buying more products, shipping demand from Asia to North America jumped. This directed more containers to North American ports. However, there was more demand for imports to the United States than for exports back to Asia, and freight carriers make more money shipping full containers than they do empty ones. Carriers were at first reluctant to make these unprofitable shipments of empty containers. By the fall of 2021, only 40 out of every 100 shipping containers that arrived in North American ports were filled up and shipped out. The remaining 60 sat empty and added to a growing inventory. Eventually, however, freight

> "In my 40 years of living and working in Southern California, I have never seen container ships off the coast of Malibu, and yet there they are, because there is no more room for them in the parking lots that are the ports of [Los Angeles] and Long Beach."[9]
>
> —Bradford Hughes, member of the Transportation & Logistics Practice at Clark Hill PLC

companies returned empty containers to Asia to meet demand. Meanwhile, the market for new containers had grown. By 2021, shipping container manufacturers were charging double the cost they had charged in 2020.[7]

Even full shipping containers caused problems. In October 2021, the Port of Savannah in Georgia, the third-largest container ship port in the United States, had nearly 80,000 shipping containers stacked in its yard and surrounding areas.[8] Some of the containers had been waiting for their owners to collect them for a full month because of COVID-19 absences and labor shortages, especially among truck drivers. Prior to the pandemic, the United States was reporting a shortage of 61,000 drivers. The American Trucking Associations in late 2021 predicted that number would rise to 160,000 in the following years because of retirements, career changes, and fewer people entering the profession.[10] A shortage of drivers and trucks meant there was no one to haul away shipping containers once they were unloaded. Those drivers who were servicing ports faced additional strain, working longer to move an increasingly large number of containers.

> ### SHIPPING CONTAINERS
> The standard shipping container revolutionized how businesses move freight around the country and around the world. It was invented by Malcolm McLean in 1956. McLean, who owned the largest US trucking company at that time, had watched dock loaders struggle with a variety of different-sized cargo containers as they were loaded into his trucks. He came up with the idea of using standard-sized containers that would protect merchandise, reduce theft, and allow for easy movement among trucks, rail cars, and ships. By the end of the century, McLean's invention was being used for most of the world's cargo.

The clog of containers awaiting transport out of the Savannah port slowed the process of unloading full ships as they arrived. At one point, more than 20 full ships were at anchor waiting to unload in a line off the coast that stretched 17 miles (27 km) into the Atlantic Ocean.[11] All these issues created significant increases in the cost of shipping. A shipment that cost $1,344 in March 2020 cost more than $11,000 by September 2021.[12]

CHAPTER SEVEN

EVERYONE HAS TO EAT

Few parts of the US economy suffered as big a disruption from the COVID-19 pandemic as the food industry. Food, agriculture, and related industries make up approximately 5 percent of the US GDP. More than one in every ten people in the United States is employed in the food and agriculture sector.[1]

Before the pandemic, Americans spent more than half of their food dollars on food eaten away from home. That amount included not only dine-in restaurants but also take-out, delivery, and food service locations such as school and workplace cafeterias. As COVID-19 cases in the United States increased, indoor dining in restaurants virtually ground to a halt. An analysis of how the restaurant industry responded to the crisis revealed three key coping strategies. The first was a pivot from in-house dining to take-out and delivery dining. Hungry Americans spent $769 billion ordering food in 2020,

To stay safe during the pandemic, people used services such as DoorDash to have meals from restaurants delivered to their homes.

GHOST KITCHENS

The pandemic-fueled growth of food delivery services such as Grubhub and DoorDash led to a new food service category called ghost kitchens. Like a restaurant, ghost kitchens offer physical spaces for food preparation. Unlike restaurants, there are no tables, no waitstaff, and no places to eat. Food prepared in ghost kitchens is accessed only through delivery services.

Ghost kitchens have provided an unexpected opportunity for new restaurateurs to get into the business. A single ghost kitchen facility may prepare dishes for multiple food businesses, including a mix of established restaurants with physical locations as well as some that offer only delivery. Some established restaurants use ghost kitchen menus to test out new dishes and see if they are popular with customers before adding them to their regular restaurants.

---

with delivery orders up 142 percent and carryout orders up 130 percent.[2]

The second strategy was to change menu offerings, hours of operation, and staffing schedules. Reduced menu offerings and reduced hours allowed restaurants to continue operating with fewer workers while leaving time for deep cleaning in off hours. Social distancing was easier for employees thanks to changes to staffing schedules. For example, employees who prepared food worked different hours than employees who served food.

A third strategy that some restaurants employed to stay open was to think differently about their space. Restaurants with available space added outdoor dining areas, including spaces specifically designed for customers

Some restaurants set up plastic bubbles around outdoor tables to further reduce the risk of the spread of COVID-19.

to enjoy takeout from the restaurants' own menus. With dining rooms closed, some restaurants used that space to expand food prep and packaging for carryout orders and add social distancing for employees. Other restaurants used newly available dining room space to create pop-up markets. These places sold key food items that were in short supply at grocery stores but were still available in restaurant supply chains.

AN EYE ON SUPPLY

The pandemic highlighted the web of businesses working behind the scenes to create restaurant and cafeteria meals, from the farms that produce the ingredients to the distributors who package and deliver them. Many restaurant owners sought creative solutions to stay in business during the pandemic, not only to maintain

> "Grocery stores are being decimated, but restaurants and their distributors are sitting on so much product that it would be a shame to not find a way to still feed our guests."[3]
>
> —André Vener, co-owner of Dog Haus restaurant

paychecks for their employees but also to keep the suppliers in business until the post–COVID-19 recovery.

Like many farms, Orchard Point Oyster Co. sold its oysters exclusively to restaurants prior to the pandemic. As restaurants closed, Orchard Point had no place to sell its oysters. The company quickly collaborated with another company to sell its oysters directly to consumers. While the volumes never reached what the company had sold to restaurants, the direct-to-consumer orders allowed them to stay in business.

Similarly, farmer-owned cooperative Land O'Lakes normally sold a large amount of butter, milk, and cheese to food service businesses. As the pandemic wiped out food service orders, the cooperative faced the prospect of dumping millions of gallons of its farmer-owners' milk unless it could find different markets. To avoid that, the company engaged directly with grocery stores to sell food service–sized packages of butter and cheese on grocery market shelves instead.

Ketchup company Heinz also grappled with changing patterns in how condiments were consumed during the pandemic. While the company had plenty of ketchup in bottles, it faced a shortage of single-serve packets as drive-through, take-out, and delivery orders replaced dine-in options.

LIVESTOCK LOSSES

The JBS pork plant in Worthington, Minnesota, processes 20,000 hogs in a normal day.[4] In April 2020, the plant was one of several around the country forced to shut down temporarily because of a COVID-19 outbreak among plant workers. Local farmers suddenly had nowhere to send their animals for harvesting.

Meat plants can accept livestock for processing only if the animals are in a specific range of weight. As the pandemic wore on, many became too large, and farmers had no choice but to euthanize the animals. Hundreds of thousands of livestock were killed and their bodies buried or composted instead of being processed into meat. The United States Department of Agriculture made payments to farmers to help them weather the loss. Despite the financial assistance, farmers still grappled with the heavy emotional toll of having to put down the very animals they had been caring for.

BUSY AISLES, EMPTY SHELVES

Grocery stores saw an almost immediate increase in business as restaurant and other food service options closed. Average US household grocery spending jumped 29 percent in March 2020 compared to February as

US COVID-19 cases began to increase. Grocery spending again rose by 20 percent from November 2020 to December 2020 as another wave of infections rippled across the nation.[5]

Pandemic-induced grocery shopping lifted virtually all segments of the industry, including smaller retailers. Consumers gravitated to those stores because of smaller crowds and the chance that hard-to-find items might still be in stock. Top-selling items in the early days of the pandemic were toilet paper, frozen food, and hand sanitizer.

Pantry staples also saw increased interest, especially in the first week of March after President Donald Trump first acknowledged the threat of the coronavirus to the nation. Sales of dried beans rose by 62.9 percent, tuna sales jumped by 31 percent, and dried milk sales increased

> ### I'M NOT EATING THAT
> Pandemic shopping put a harsh spotlight on which foods most consumers did or did not want to buy when they had to eat at home. Some shoppers were quick to pick up on these trends and share their own observations and photos on social media. Multiple Twitter posts showed virtually empty shelves and coolers with just one unwanted item remaining. Such leftover items included things like chocolate hummus, pineapple pizza, and plant-based hot dogs. These posts injected a slice of humor into an otherwise frightening time.

by 126.3 percent as consumers stocked up on supplies in preparation for an extended stay at home.[6]

Not all food categories saw increases as consumers spent more time and money on cooking at home. Early in the pandemic, there was a drop in sales of fresh fruits and vegetables. Consumers avoided buying them for fear someone else had touched them or because they felt fresh produce would not last as long as processed or frozen food items. As consumers became more comfortable with masks, social distancing, and other safety measures, sales of fresh fruits and vegetables returned to normal levels.

LASTING IMPACT

In addition to changing what they were buying, the pandemic changed how consumers were buying. More consumers turned to digital tools to reduce the number of store trips they made or limit the amount of time they spent in the stores. As more grocery stores offered online ordering, pickup, or delivery, consumers took greater advantage of those services as well.

By the end of 2020, spending on food eaten away from home had dropped. Some 55 percent of consumers

MEAL KIT REVIVAL

Sales of meal kits, which offer home delivery of the items needed to make a particular recipe, spiked during the pandemic. Consumers said they appreciated the safety and convenience of kits coming to their doors. Many meal kit customers also reported enjoying the process of cooking homemade meals. Prior to the pandemic, the meal kit industry struggled to keep customers because of the cost of the product. Meal kits were cheaper than a restaurant-delivered meal, but they were still more expensive than buying the same ingredients from a grocery store. After the pandemic, meal kit companies were counting on more people continuing to cook at home even if kits cost a little more.

reported that they were eating at home more often than they had in the past. These consumers reported that breakfasts eaten at home rose from 33 to 44 percent, lunches at home increased from 18 to 31 percent, and dinners eaten at home increased from 21 to 33 percent compared with pre-pandemic times.[7]

In December 2020, marketing communications firm HUNTER surveyed consumers about their future food plans. More than 70 percent of people who began to cook at home more often due to the pandemic said they planned to continue cooking more at home even after the pandemic ended. More than 80 percent of the home cooks said they had found enjoyment in cooking and baking.[8] Home cooks also ate together as a family more often.

Another trend that has remained after the pandemic lockdowns is online grocery shopping. A summer 2021 study by sales and marketing company Acosta found that 45 percent of consumers surveyed had increased their online grocery shopping. The survey also showed that 45 percent of those ordering online were using home delivery, and those driving to the store to pick up purchases were favoring curbside over in-store pickup.[9]

Many people discovered a love of preparing food at home during the pandemic.

CHAPTER EIGHT

MOVING UP, MOVING OUT

The COVID-19 pandemic led millions of Americans to relocate. A June 2020 survey found that around one in every five adults either changed where they lived during the pandemic or knew someone who did.[1] For some, this meant moving in with someone else or having someone move in with them. For others, it meant finding a different place to live, either to rent or to buy.

The pandemic significantly impacted the US residential real estate market. It changed where people wanted to live. It affected what types of homes they wanted to live in. It led to dramatic increases in the price of available homes and a surge in demand during a time of restricted supply. For many who did not move, they increased spending to upgrade their current homes. For those already having a difficult time making

Some people who lived alone grew bored or lonely. Many of these people chose to move in with others to avoid isolation.

> "I started to feel really lonely in my apartment by myself, and I just kind of felt trapped."[3]
> —Anna Johnson, who moved back in with her parents during the pandemic

rent or mortgage payments, the pandemic created a crisis and fears of eviction.

The COVID-19 pandemic made an existing shortage of homes and affordable housing even more pronounced. It created new opportunities for some people to live in different places even as it made it more difficult for others to live in their current homes. It also changed the way people buy and sell houses.

BUST TO BOOM

Residential real estate appeared to be yet another victim of the COVID-19 pandemic in the early months of 2020. New listings of homes for sale were down 40 percent in April 2020 from April 2019 as homeowners elected to stay in place because of health concerns or concerns about the economy.[2] But by May, more people were searching for properties. By the summer of 2020, home sales were nearing their pre-pandemic levels, yet the supply of homes available for purchase remained low. This led to intense competition and bidding for a small number of homes among a larger number of buyers. In June 2021, the average price for an existing home in the United States had risen 24.3 percent from the previous year.[4]

The types and locations of sought-after homes also changed. Many consumers with big enough budgets opted for large suburban homes with features such as dedicated home office spaces and swimming pools. Others left large urban areas for smaller ones. Consumers who were able to work remotely had more

MORE FOREVER HOMES

The COVID-19 pandemic meant more people had time to introduce a pet into their homes. A study by the American Pet Products Association found that more than 12 million US households got a pet after the pandemic began.[5] In addition, animal shelters reported that fewer people surrendered their pets, meaning there was a lower number of available animals, and a higher percentage of those were placed in homes. As people spent more time with their pets, they also became more aware of how those pets were feeling. They spent more on pet supplies and veterinary care, causing those industries to grow. Meanwhile, animal health companies and pet supply retailers, including Chewy.com, posted healthy gains. But the growing number of pets led to stress and burnout for workers at many veterinary clinics, which were already short-staffed.

REALTORS RETOOL

Fears of infection led to dramatic changes in how Americans bought and sold houses during the pandemic. Some real estate agents used Facebook Live events instead of in-person showings to virtually walk potential buyers through properties. Others met clients in person, though everyone wore masks, gloves, and foot covers. Virtual reality home tours complete with integrated video chats also became an option for buyers. Such options made it possible for buyers to find, buy, and close on a home without ever setting foot in it.

choices in where they could move.

LUMBER SHORTAGES

Unlike the Great Recession (2007–2009), which came at a time of overbuilding, the COVID-19 pandemic came during a time of underbuilding. This meant that more people wanted houses or apartments to buy or rent than were available. In June 2021, the National Association of Realtors estimated the United States was short at least 5.5 million housing units.[6] This shortage, the group said, drove rent increases and increases in the prices of available homes. At the same time, mortgage rates, or the cost of borrowing money to buy a home, were at historic lows. At the start of the pandemic, the interest rate on a 30-year fixed-rate mortgage was 3.45 percent. By July 2020, it had fallen to 2.87 percent. That amounted to a $100-a-month savings on a median-priced home.[7]

Some people chose to move from apartments to houses with yards so they could have their own outdoor space. This caused vacancies in apartments.

As prices for existing homes jumped, some buyers considered new construction. The COVID-19 pandemic stalled that option as construction work halted amid fears of disease outbreaks. In March 2020, there were more than 1,160,000 construction projects for new housing units, but in April, that number dropped to 891,000.[8]

Those numbers sent warning signals throughout the lumber and home construction industries. Fearing a long-term slowdown and seeking to protect employees,

The high cost of lumber made new homes more expensive to build.

lumber producers temporarily shut down production to add new COVID-19 safety protocols. In the meantime, lumber demand took an unexpected upswing as homeowners began expanding or improving their homes. This imbalance in supply and demand for places to live led to shortages of construction materials, especially lumber. Higher lumber prices alone tacked an additional $35,872 onto the cost of a new single-family home built in the spring of 2021.[9]

CHALLENGES FOR RENTERS

Many first-time home buyers during the pandemic were moving from renting to owning. Along with a trend of people moving in with friends or family, this led to a slight easing in rental rates as more vacancies occurred. This was especially the case in traditionally high-rent cities such as San Francisco and New York City.

Despite this slight decrease in rent, many renters, especially renters of color, faced a different situation. A US Census Bureau analysis found that 66 percent of renters of color were having difficulty paying rent in the fall of 2021.[10] Renters of color were more

HOTELS FOR THE HOMELESS

People experiencing homelessness, many of whom suffer from pre-existing medical conditions, were especially vulnerable to COVID-19. Some US cities moved homeless individuals from crowded shelters to empty hotels to reduce infection rates. Tens of thousands of homeless people found a temporary respite from the streets thanks to emergency federal funding. As the funding ran out, some cities bought old hotels to use as permanent solutions. Others turned people back out onto the streets. In some cases, however, a hotel stay turned out to be a turning point. Hennepin County, Minnesota, was able to move homeless people from the hotels to permanent housing. Social workers said the stability of the hotel housing allowed some people to pick up additional jobs. It was also easier for people to access mental and physical health resources.

AVOIDING EVICTIONS

Evictions were a concern long before COVID-19. When the pandemic hit, however, many state and local leaders felt it was more important than ever to keep people in their homes. Researchers from Princeton University's Eviction Lab had some ideas on how to do that. One idea was to use online court hearings to reduce case backlogs. Another was for elected leaders to increase the availability of temporary rental assistance. Mediation services to get tenants and landlords talking before going to court also had been shown to reduce evictions. The city of Philadelphia, Pennsylvania, began requiring tenants and landlords to talk things through, including making a payment plan, before filing with the court. That program helped avoid evictions in most cases from 2020 to the end of 2021.

likely to experience pandemic-related job losses. In addition, high-rent urban areas such as New York City and Los Angeles and San Francisco in California also experienced some of the highest rates of COVID-19 and related job losses in the country. Low-income renters in those markets already had challenges paying their rent. Pandemic-related job losses made it even harder.

While Congress had authorized aid to help low-income renters, delivering the aid proved to be slow and complex. The CARES Act included a ban on evictions for nonpayment of rent from March 27, 2020, through July 24, 2020. The CDC also issued its own eviction moratorium

Some people protested evictions in New York City in August 2021 as moratoriums ended.

beginning September 4, 2020, to help reduce the spread of COVID-19. It was lifted on August 26, 2021, in all but a handful of states.

By the end of the moratorium, an estimated 11 million renters were behind on their payments. Some 3.6 million households were at risk of losing their homes due to eviction.[11] Many landlords also faced missing mortgage payments on the rental units they managed. A survey of property owners in December 2020 found a majority anticipated financial stress from missed mortgage payments, late payments of property taxes, and inadequate cash flow to pay for property repairs and upkeep.

CHAPTER NINE

HEALTH-CARE BILLS

COVID-19 sent more than three million Americans to the hospital between August 2020 and November 2021 alone. Meanwhile, hospitals recorded a significant decline in admissions for conditions other than COVID-19 during the same period. In April 2020, non–COVID-19 admissions decreased by more than 40 percent as hospitals discouraged noncritical procedures in order to free up beds and staff to handle the surge of COVID-19 cases.[1] Even by the summer of 2020, as the number of cases decreased, non–COVID-19 hospital visits were still down by 20 percent from pre-pandemic levels. This led to the first year of reduced health-care spending since 1960.

Business dropped 12 percent for dental care as patients avoided routine or noncritical procedures for fear of infection. Nursing home spending dropped 5 percent as outbreaks caused potential residents to

Because they were worried about getting COVID-19, some people avoided seeking health care for issues not related to COVID-19 when they needed it.

seek other care options. Routine doctor visits also were down by 2 percent compared with prior years.[2] These decreases led to thousands of layoffs and furloughs of health-care workers.

Those workers who did remain faced long shifts, high stress, and burnout. A national survey of nurses in early 2021 found 51 percent said they had felt exhausted within the two weeks preceding the survey, and 43 percent said

Many health-care workers experienced long periods of stress as they struggled to help patients with COVID-19.

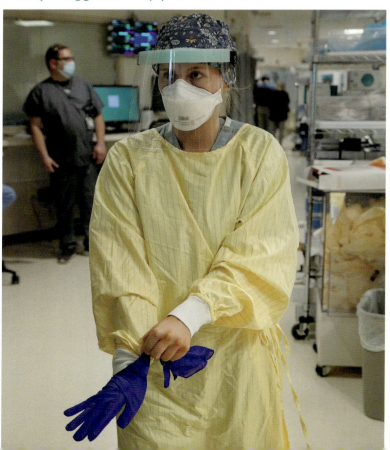

they had felt overwhelmed during that same time. Nearly four in ten surveyed said they either intended to leave their jobs or were thinking about leaving their jobs within the next six months.[3]

LONG-TERM CONCERNS

Health-care providers can estimate how much the pandemic has cost the industry in lost jobs, burned-out workers, and reductions in patients seeking preventive or elective care. It's less clear what the economic impact of those losses will be in the future. At the height of the early pandemic, health-care employment was down nearly 10 percent. It rebounded over time, but more than a year later, it was still down 3 percent from pre-pandemic levels.[4]

Some analysts argued that businesses must trim their employee numbers when business is down, and that health care is no exception. As patients continue to hold off on seeking health-care services, health-care executives are asking if more people are viewing health services as a luxury good instead of a necessity. That change alone could force the health-care system to become smaller, more efficient, and less costly.

At the same time, avoiding doctor and hospital visits for some health conditions leads to bigger problems in the future. For example, hospital admissions for strokes and heart attacks were down from normal levels during the pandemic. While patients may have avoided seeking care due to infection concerns, delaying this care may have worsened their health. Some research indicates there were more deaths from conditions not related to COVID-19 than would be normal. In addition, some people who became sick with COVID-19 report ongoing health challenges even after they tested negative. This situation, referred to as long COVID, may require ongoing care that would not have been needed prior to the pandemic.

> ### NECESSITY AND INVENTION
>
> Shortages of masks, ventilators, and personal protective equipment for health-care workers led to some creative solutions in the pandemic's early days. Innovative businesses created adapters to turn snorkeling masks into ventilators and to make common CPAP machines, used to treat sleep apnea, into less-invasive breathing solutions for COVID-19 patients. Another innovation created openings in masks for eating. Electronics giant LG developed a battery-powered face mask with dual air purifiers and a special case that disinfected the mask with ultraviolet light after it was worn.

NEW NORMAL

Few industries escaped the economic impact of COVID-19. Whether they profited or were pummeled, the pandemic forced many businesses to change their operations. Some of those changes will be permanent. Automation will continue to erode face-to-face work and jobs requiring relatively little training. Teleconferencing and other internet-based technologies will enable wider and more convenient access to health-care providers, online retailers, and a variety of entertainment options. Public transit systems and core downtown businesses that relied on suburban commuters may never recover from a permanent shift to more work-from-home models. Business travel is unlikely ever to reach pre-pandemic levels as more meetings move online.

TRASHED

The recycling and reusable materials businesses were among the industries that suffered during COVID-19. Because they feared that the virus could be transmitted from surfaces, many people dumped materials that otherwise would have been recycled. Those fears also led to mountains of personal protective equipment, such as surgical masks and gowns, being misclassified as hazardous waste. Hazardous waste cannot go in the trash, so it often ends up as litter or gets burned. Infection fears also slowed operations at recycling businesses, which added to the problem.

Likewise, governments around the world will be dealing with the economic impact of the pandemic for years. Global governments racked up $11 trillion in debt in 2020 to help their economies weather the COVID-19 storm.[5] This borrowing will come at the expense of other government priorities. In the meantime, policymakers, businesses, and consumers are acknowledging the important role these fiscal policies played in reducing the pandemic's economic impact.

Businesses are re-evaluating the way they run their supply chains. The push toward globalization, where businesses seek suppliers or partners beyond their own borders, is expected to slow. They may prefer suppliers closer to home, especially for important goods such as ventilators, masks, and food.

The pandemic also caused inflation. Prices in October 2021 averaged 6.2 percent higher than in October 2020. It was the largest jump in inflation in 30 years.[6] The COVID-19 pandemic fueled these price increases because people had stimulus money to spend while temporary business shutdowns, supply chain snags, and labor issues made products and services harder to come by.

GENERATIONAL CHANGES

The COVID-19 pandemic represented a significant loss of life and a loss of economic productivity. It also reflected the ability of businesses, governments, and consumers to adapt and change to new realities. In the case of businesses, such challenges can lead to innovations that might otherwise have taken far longer or might never have occurred.

COVID-19 accelerated innovation in artificial intelligence (AI) as a replacement for in-person contact. AI is a machine's simulation of human intelligence. Young people beginning their careers are finding more opportunities for jobs maintaining these technologies,

HACKERS TAKE AIM AT VACCINE SUPPLIES

In late 2020, IBM Security researchers discovered a hacking campaign targeting sensitive information about vaccine distribution. The hackers targeted companies across Europe, North and South America, and Asia. Analysts said the hackers seemed to be trying to disrupt or destroy vaccine supplies so that people would not trust the vaccines. The attacks began with a phishing email that sought to gain usernames and passwords of people at different places along the vaccine supply chain. Phishing is when hackers send emails pretending to be someone else in order to gain sensitive information from the recipient.

yet it has come at a price. Industries that previously focused on face-to-face contact, including travel, leisure, and hospitality, laid off workers in the race to replace those positions with technology. The millions of individuals who held those primarily low-wage jobs were disproportionately women and people of color.

Companies have developed delivery robots that bring food orders to people's homes.

Jerome Powell commented on this challenge in August 2021. He said, "It may be that some of these people will have a harder time finding their way back in to the workforce without more education and training. . . . That's a part of the recovery that's far from complete." Powell added that the COVID-19 pandemic may one day be viewed as a historical event that forever altered how the students of that time saw the world: "This is an extraordinary time and I believe that it will result in an extraordinary generation."[7]

> "We're not simply going back to the economy that we had before the pandemic."[8]
>
> —Jerome Powell, chair of the Federal Reserve Board

ESSENTIAL FACTS

KEY EVENTS

- The Dow Jones Industrial Average drops nearly 3,000 points on March 16, 2020, losing almost 13 percent of its value. It is the worst day for the Dow since the 1929 stock market crash.

- The US Department of Labor reports that 3.28 million Americans filed initial unemployment claims in the week ending March 21, 2020, which at the time is the largest number since modern figures began being tracked in 1967.

- President Donald Trump signs the nearly $2 trillion Coronavirus Aid, Relief, and Economic Security (CARES) Act on March 27, 2020.

- According to the National Bureau of Economic Research, the COVID-19 recession lasted from February to April 2020.

- The unemployment rate for April 2020 rises to 14.8 percent, the highest unemployment rate since record keeping began in 1948.

KEY PEOPLE

- Donald Trump served as US president in the first year of the COVID-19 pandemic and signed multiple pieces of legislation meant to bolster the distressed economy.

- Jerome Powell is chair of the Federal Reserve Board, which is charged with maintaining financial stability in the US economy, among other tasks.

- Speaker of the US House of Representatives Nancy Pelosi oversaw efforts to get House approval of COVID-19 relief legislation that had been approved by the Senate to deliver it for President Trump's signature.

- US Senate majority leader Mitch McConnell oversaw Senate efforts to create legislation during the pandemic to help individuals, businesses, and state and local governments make it through the worst economic impacts.

KEY STATISTICS

- Online sales increased from 16 percent of all sales in 2019 to nearly 20 percent in 2020.
- Prices for goods averaged 6.2 percent higher in October 2021 than in October 2020. This was the largest rate of inflation in 30 years.
- Retail sales in April 2020 fell 14.3 percent from their March 2020 level.
- Approximately 56 percent of the jobs lost between February 2020 and September 2021 were in the lowest-paying industries, even though those industries represented just 30 percent of all jobs.
- For the period from April through June 2020, GDP dropped at an annualized rate of more than 31 percent, the largest drop in US history.
- In April 2020 alone, the COVID-19 pandemic led to the loss of some 20.5 million jobs.

QUOTE

"The normalcy we called pre-COVID, that no longer exists. We have to be prepared, on our toes, to adapt."

—Lyle Richardson, chief operating officer of A. Marshall Hospitality

GLOSSARY

automation
The technology that enables tasks to be performed without human assistance.

economy
A system in which things are ranked by value and exchanged.

euthanize
To purposely and humanely end the life of an animal.

eviction
When someone is forced out of a home or apartment, often because of nonpayment of rent or mortgage bills.

fiscal policy
The decisions a government makes to control its spending and taxation, including considering the impact of those decisions on the larger economy.

freight
Goods carried by planes, ships, trains, or trucks.

furlough
A temporary unpaid leave of absence or time off from work, often for a set period of time.

gross domestic product (GDP)
The monetary value of all final goods and services produced within a nation's geographic borders over a specified period of time.

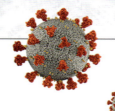

index
An evaluation of the change in a large group of things by analyzing the changes in a smaller representative group.

inventory
A complete list of items that a store has for sale.

moratorium
An authorized suspension of an activity or the payment of a debt.

ratio
A comparison of two numbers using division.

retail sales
Purchases by consumers of finished goods and services.

revenue
Income, especially of a company or organization.

service
An instance in which a consumer pays others to provide a benefit, such as a haircut.

stimulus
Something that prompts further activity.

trade association
A group that represents multiple businesses in the same industry and works to promote their common interests.

ADDITIONAL RESOURCES

SELECTED BIBLIOGRAPHY

"Tracking the COVID-19 Economy's Effects on Food, Housing and Employment Hardships." *Center on Budget and Policy Priorities*, 10 Nov. 2021, cbpp.org. Accessed 10 Dec. 2021.

Wu, Nicholas, and Javier Zarracina. "All of the COVID-19 Stimulus Bills, Visualized." *USA Today*, 11 Mar. 2021, usatoday.com. Accessed 10 Dec. 2021.

Yeyati, Eduardo Levy, and Federico Filippini. "Social and Economic Impact of COVID-19." *Brookings Institution*, 8 June 2021, brookings.edu. Accessed 10 Dec. 2021.

FURTHER READINGS

Davis, Kenneth C. *More Deadly than War: The Hidden History of the Spanish Flu and the First World War*. Henry Holt, 2018.

Edwards, Sue Bradford. *Coronavirus: The COVID-19 Pandemic*. Abdo, 2021.

Henzel, Cynthia Kennedy. *Society and Culture during COVID-19*. Abdo, 2023.

ONLINE RESOURCES

To learn more about the economic impact of COVID-19, please visit **abdobooklinks.com** or scan this QR code. These links are routinely monitored and updated to provide the most current information available.

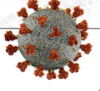

MORE INFORMATION

For more information on this subject, contact or visit the following organizations:

BROOKINGS INSTITUTION

1775 Massachusetts Ave. NW
Washington, DC 20036
202-797-6000
brookings.edu

The Brookings Institution is a nonprofit public policy organization based in Washington, DC. During the COVID-19 pandemic, Brookings focused on conducting in-depth research aimed at helping policymakers protect lives and save livelihoods.

UNIVERSITY OF CHICAGO BOOTH SCHOOL OF BUSINESS

5807 S. Woodlawn Ave.
Chicago, IL 60637
773-702-7743
chicagobooth.edu

This website features the latest faculty COVID-19 observations and insights on the global health crisis. Visitors also can learn how the University of Chicago Booth School of Business community is addressing the pandemic's impact on businesses.

SOURCE NOTES

CHAPTER 1. UNPRECEDENTED AID

1. Jim Zarroli and Avie Schneider. "3.3 Million File Unemployment Claims." *NPR*, 26 Mar. 2020, npr.org. Accessed 30 Mar. 2022.
2. Emily Cochrane and Nicholas Fandos. "Senate Approves $2 Trillion Stimulus after Bipartisan Deal." *New York Times*, 5 May 2020, nytimes.com. Accessed 30 Mar. 2022.
3. Nicholas Wu and Javier Zarracina. "All of the COVID-19 Stimulus Bills, Visualized." *USA Today*, 17 Mar. 2021, usatoday.com. Accessed 30 Mar. 2022.
4. "The $2 Trillion CARES Act, a Response to COVID-19, Is Equivalent to 45% of All 2019 Federal Spending." *USAFacts*, 23 Sept. 2020, usafacts.org. Accessed 30 Mar. 2022.
5. "How Does COVID Relief Compare to Great Recession Stimulus?" *Committee for a Responsible Federal Budget*, 1 July 2020, crfb.org. Accessed 30 Mar. 2022.
6. "CARES Act Includes $250 Billion for Unemployment Benefits." *Waller*, 26 Mar. 2020, wallerlaw.com. Accessed 30 Mar. 2022.
7. David Slotnick. "Airlines Will Get the $60 Billion Bailout They Asked For." *Insider*, 27 Mar. 2020, businessinsider.com. Accessed 30 Mar. 2022.
8. Jacob Pramuk. "Trump Signs $2 Trillion Coronavirus Relief Bill." *CNBC*, 28 Mar. 2020, cnbc.com. Accessed 30 Mar. 2022.
9. Ryan Lucas. "DOJ Has Charged Nearly 500 with COVID-Related Fraud in the Past Year." *NPR*, 26 Mar. 2021, npr.org. Accessed 30 Mar. 2022.
10. Zarroli and Schneider, "3.3 Million File Unemployment Claims."

CHAPTER 2. COVID-19 RECESSION

1. David John Marotta. "Longest Economic Expansion in United States History." *Forbes*, 21 Jan. 2020, forbes.com. Accessed 30 Mar. 2022.
2. Sergei Klebnikov. "Here's How 2019 Turned Out to Be a Historic Year for the Stock Market." *Forbes*, 1 Jan. 2020, forbes.com. Accessed 30 Mar. 2022.
3. Will Feuer. "US Coronavirus Cases Surpass 1,000, Up Nearly Ten-Fold in a Week." *CNBC*, 11 Mar. 2020, cnbc.com. Accessed 30 Mar. 2022.
4. Jonathan Garber. "Dow Plunges over 2,000 Points." *Fox Business*, 9 Mar. 2020, foxbusiness.com. Accessed 13 Apr. 2022.
5. Alain Sherter. "Weekly Jobless Claims Fall to Pandemic Low as Labor Market Continues to Heal." *CBS News*, 20 May 2021, cbsnews.com. Accessed 30 March 2022.
6. "GDP: One of the Great Inventions of the 20th Century." *Bureau of Economic Analysis*, n.d. apps.bea.gov. Accessed 30 Mar. 2022.
7. Kimberly Amadeo. "How Does the 2020 Stock Market Crash Compare With Others?" *The Balance*, 31 Oct. 2021, thebalance.com. Accessed 30 Mar. 2022.
8. Amadeo, "How Does the 2020 Stock Market Crash Compare?"
9. Tracy Hadden Loh and Joanne Kim. "To Recover from COVID-19, Downtowns Must Adapt." *Brookings*, 15 Apr. 2021, brookings.edu. Accessed 30 Mar. 2022.
10. Laura Wronski. "CNBC|SurveyMonkey Small Business Index Q2 2020." *SurveyMonkey*, n.d., surveymonkey.com. Accessed 30 Mar. 2022.
11. Christina Capatides. "These Workers Are Going Without Pay During the Coronavirus Crisis." *CBS News*, 19 Mar. 2020, cbsnews.com. Accessed 30 Mar. 2022.
12. "Unemployment Rates During the COVID-19 Pandemic." *Congressional Research Service*, 20 Aug. 2021, sgp.fas.org. Accessed 30 Mar. 2022.
13. US Bureau of Labor Statistics. "Average Weekly Hours of Production." *Federal Reserve Bank of St. Louis*, n.d., fred.stlouisfed.org. Accessed 30 Mar. 2022.
14. Peter Caputo et al. "Return to a World Transformed." *Deloitte*, 2 Aug. 2021, deloitte.com. Accessed 30 Mar. 2022.
15. "Global Consumer Confidence Suffers Record Drop in Q2." *Cision*, 15 July 2020, prnewswire.com. Accessed 30 Mar. 2022.
16. "US Economy Plunges 31.4% in the Second Quarter but a Big Rebound Is Expected." *CNBC*, 30 Sept. 2020, cnbc.com. Accessed 30 Mar. 2022.

CHAPTER 3. LABOR IN THE SPOTLIGHT

1. Jeff Cox. "A Record 20.5 Million Jobs Were Lost in April as Unemployment Rate Jumps to 14.7%." *CNBC*, 8 May 2020, cnbc.com. Accessed 30 Mar. 2022.
2. "Unemployment Rates During the COVID-19 Pandemic." *Congressional Research Service*, 20 Aug. 2021, sgp.fas.org. Accessed 30 Mar. 2022.
3. Diana Boesch and Shilpa Phadke. "When Women Lose All the Jobs." *CAP*, 1 Feb. 2021, americanprogress.org. Accessed 30 Mar. 2022.
4. "Labor Force Statistics from the Current Population Survey." *US BLS*, n.d., bls.gov. Accessed 30 Mar. 2022.
5. Jonathan Rothwell. "Official Jobless Figures Will Miss the Economic Pain of the Pandemic." *Brookings*, 3 April 2020, brookings.edu. Accessed 30 Mar. 2022.
6. Jennifer Harper. "The Uneven Race to Economic Recovery." *University of Miami*, 31 Oct. 2021, race-and-social-justice-review.law.miami.edu. Accessed 30 Mar. 2022.
7. "Unemployment Rates During the COVID-19 Pandemic."
8. Hye Jin Rho, Hayley Brown, and Shawn Fremstad. "A Basic Demographic Profile of Workers in Frontline Industries." *CEPR*, April 2020, cepr.net. Accessed 30 Mar. 2022.
9. Alyssa Fowers and Shelly Tan. "The New Sick Leave Law." *Washington Post*, 19 Mar. 2020, washingtonpost.com. Accessed 30 Mar. 2022.
10. Paul Wiseman. "Economic Oddity: Record Job Openings and Many Unemployed." *Associated Press*, 8 Sept. 2021, apnews.com. Accessed 30 Mar. 2022.
11. Wiseman, "Economic Oddity."
12. "COVID-19 and the Rise of the Digital Nomad." *MBO Partners*, n.d., s29814.pcdn.co. Accessed 30 Mar. 2022.
13. Elaina Patton. "As Office Life Beckons Again, the Pandemic's Digital Nomads Weigh Benefits." *NBC News*, 6 July 2021, nbcnews.com. Accessed 30 Mar. 2022.
14. Patrick Coate. "Remote Work Before, During, and After the Pandemic." *NCCI*, 25 Jan. 2021, ncci.com. Accessed 30 Mar. 2022.
15. Sarah Jackson. "2 out of 3 Americans Say They Would Take a Pay Cut to Work Remotely Full Time." *Insider*, 3 Aug. 2021, businessinsider.com. Accessed 30 Mar. 2022.

CHAPTER 4. SHUTTERED DOORS

1. Diego Mendez-Carbajo. "Consumer Spending and the Pandemic." *Federal Reserve Bank of St. Louis*, Jan. 2021, research.stlouisfed.org. Accessed 30 Mar. 2022.
2. Jacob Roshgadol. "Quarter of Gym-Goers Don't Expect They'll Ever Return to Fitness Clubs." *Study Finds*, 30 June 2020, studyfinds.org. Accessed 30 Mar. 2022.
3. Mendez-Carbajo, "Consumer Spending and the COVID-19 Pandemic."
4. "September 2020 US Airline Traffic Data." *Bureau of Transportation Statistics*, 10 Dec. 2020, bts.gov. Accessed 30 Mar. 2022.
5. Cortney L. Norris et al. "Pivot! How the Restaurant Industry Adapted." *Emerald Insight*, 15 Dec. 2021, emerald.com. Accessed 30 Mar. 2022.
6. Tim Smart. "Winners and Losers of the COVID-19 Pandemic." *US News*, 24 Dec. 2020, usnews.com. Accessed 30 Mar. 2022.
7. Leland D. Crane et al. "Business Exit during the COVID-19 Pandemic." *Federal Reserve Board*, Apr. 2021, federalreserve.gov. Accessed 30 Mar. 2022.
8. Smart, "Winners and Losers."
9. Morgan Hines. "'Devastating Impact': Cruise Industry." *USA Today*, 19 Nov. 2020, usatoday.com. Accessed 30 Mar. 2022.
10. "Pandemic Impact Leads to Rental Car Shortages." *Travel Incorporated*, Mar. 2021, travelinc.com. Accessed 30 Mar. 2022.
11. "Average Air Fares Dropped to All-Time Low in 2020." *Bureau of Transportation Statistics*, 20 Apr. 2021, bts.gov. Accessed 30 Mar. 2022.
12. Mae Anderson and Tom Krisher. "As Workers Stay at Home Due to COVID, Downtown Businesses Adjust to a New Reality." *Fortune*, 13 Sept. 2021, fortune.com. Accessed 30 Mar. 2022.
13. Alexander W. Bartik et al. "The Impact of COVID-19 on Small Business Outcomes and Expectations." *PNAS*, 10 July 2020, pnas.org. Accessed 30 Mar. 2022.

SOURCE NOTES CONTINUED

14. Akrur Barua and Monali Samaddar. "A Recovery in Retail Sales is Underway." *Deloitte*, 25 Sept. 2020, deloitte.com. Accessed 30 Mar. 2022.

CHAPTER 5. BOOM TIMES

1. Fareeha Ali. "Charts: How the Coronavirus Is Changing Ecommerce." *Digital Commerce 360*, 19 Feb. 2021, digitalcommerce360.com. Accessed 31 Mar. 2022.
2. Tim Smart. "Winners and Losers of the COVID-19 Pandemic." *US News*, 24 Dec. 2020, usnews.com. Accessed 31 Mar. 2022
3. Smart, "Winners and Losers."
4. Saskia Lindsay. "Video Game Industry Continues to Boom Even as COVID-19 Restrictions Lifted." *ABC News 4*, 8 July 2021, abcnews4.com. Accessed 31 Mar. 2022.
5. Noah Smith. "The Giants of the Video Game Industry Have Thrived." *Washington Post*, 12 May 2020, washingtonpost.com. Accessed 31 Mar. 2022.
6. Mike Snider. "Netflix, Amazon Prime, Disney+ and Hulu Are Streaming Favorites." *USA Today*, 16 Feb. 2021, usatoday.com. Accessed 31 Mar. 2022.
7. Smith, "The Giants of the Video Game Industry."
8. Tom Warren. "Microsoft Thinks Coronavirus Will Forever Change the Way We Work and Learn." *The Verge*, 9 Apr. 2020, theverge.com. Accessed 31 Mar. 2022.
9. Rebecca Stropoli. "Are We Really More Productive Working from Home?" *Chicago Booth Review*, 18 Aug. 2021, chicagobooth.edu. Accessed 31 Mar. 2022.
10. Kevin Stankiewicz. "Etsy CEO Says 20,000 of Its Shops Are Now Selling Face Masks." *CNBC*, 8 Apr. 2020, cnbc.com. Accessed 31 Mar. 2022.
11. Julia Kollewe. "From Pfizer to Moderna: Who's Making Billions from COVID-19 Vaccines." *Guardian*, 6 Mar. 2021, theguardian.com. Accessed 31 Mar. 2022.
12. C. Textor. "Growth Rate of Real Gross Domestic Product (GDP) in China from 2011 to 2021." *Statista*, 16 Feb. 2022, statista.com. Accessed 31 Mar. 2022.
13. "China's Economy Grows 18.3% in Post-COVID Comeback." *BBC*, 16 Apr. 2021, bbc.com. Accessed 31 Mar. 2022.
14. Rebecca Robbins and Peter S. Goodman. "Pfizer Reaps Hundreds of Millions in Profits." *New York Times*, 4 May 2021, nytimes.com. Accessed 31 Mar. 2022.
15. Daniela Sirtori-Cortina. "COVID, Wildfires Spell Big Business for Air Purifier Industry." *Seattle Times*, 9 Aug. 2021, seattletimes.com. Accessed 31 Mar. 2022.

CHAPTER 6. BREAKS IN THE CHAIN

1. Jen Wieczner. "The Case of the Missing Toilet Paper." *Fortune*, 18 May 2020, fortune.com. Accessed 31 Mar. 2022.
2. Annie Palmer. "Amazon Sellers Fined for Price Gouging Hand Sanitizer amid Coronavirus Pandemic." *CNBC*, 17 Nov. 2020, cnbc.com. Accessed 31 Mar. 2022.
3. "Economic News Release." *US BLS*, 12 May 2021, bls.gov. Accessed 31 Mar. 2022.
4. Jack Ewing and Neal E. Boudette. "A Tiny Part's Big Ripple." *New York Times*, 14 Oct. 2021, nytimes.com. Accessed 31 Mar. 2022.
5. Anne Sraders and Lance Lambert. "What to Expect in the 2022 Used Car Market." *Fortune*, 1 Nov. 2021, fortune.com. Accessed 31 Mar. 2022.
6. Michael Corkery. "'Everything Going the Wrong Way.'" *New York Times*, 30 Sept. 2021, nytimes.com. Accessed 31 Mar. 2022.
7. Ben van der Merwe. "Weekly Data: How COVID-19 Disrupted Global Shipping." *Investment Monitor*, 13 Sept. 2021, investmentmonitor.ai. Accessed 31 Mar. 2022.
8. Peter S. Goodman. "'It's Not Sustainable': What America's Port Crisis Looks Like Up Close." *New York Times*, 14 Oct. 2021, nytimes.com. Accessed 31 Mar. 2022.
9. Chandler Ford et al. "How COVID-19 Is Impacting Global Supply Chains." *National Law Review*, vol. XII, no. 90, 21 Oct. 2021, natlawreview.com. Accessed 31 Mar. 2022.
10. Bob Costello and Alan Karickhoff. "Truck Driver Shortage Analysis 2019." *American Trucking Associations*, July 2019, trucking.org. Accessed 31 Mar. 2022.
11. Goodman, "'It's Not Sustainable.'"
12. Van der Merwe, "Weekly Data: How COVID-19 Disrupted Global Shipping."

CHAPTER 7. EVERYONE HAS TO EAT

1. Frances Dillard. "The Ongoing Impact of COVID-19 on How We Shop and Eat." *Forbes*, 30 Aug. 2021, forbes.com. Accessed 31 Mar. 2022.
2. S. Lock. "Growth of Digital Restaurant Food Orders in the United States." *Statista*, 4 June 2021, statista.com. Accessed 31 Mar. 2022.
3. Alicia Kelso. "Some Restaurants Are Transforming into Markets to Survive the Coronavirus Crisis." *Forbes*, 23 Mar. 2020, forbes.com. Accessed 31 Mar. 2022.
4. "Healthy Pigs Being Killed as Meatpacking Backlog Hits Farms." *MPR News*, 1 May 2020, mprnews.org. Accessed 31 Mar. 2022.
5. Michael Browne. "By the Numbers: Looking at Sales Trends." *Supermarket News,* 15 Mar. 2021, supermarketnews.com. Accessed 31 Mar. 2022.
6. Megan Poinski. "Coronavirus Concerns Drive Huge Sales Growth for Pantry Staples." *Industry Dive*, 17 Mar. 2020, fooddive.com. Accessed 31 Mar. 2022.
7. Browne, "By the Numbers: Looking at Sales Trends"
8. "America Keeps on Cooking." *Cision*, 14 Jan. 2021, prnewswire.com. Accessed 31 Mar. 2022.
9. Russel Redman. "Increased Use of Online Grocery Shopping 'Here to Stay.'" *Supermarket News,* 25 Aug. 2021, supermarketnews.com. Accessed 31 Mar. 2022.

CHAPTER 8. MOVING UP, MOVING OUT

1. D'Vera Cohn. "About a Fifth of US Adults Moved." *Pew Research Center*, 6 July 2020, pewresearch.org. Accessed 31 Mar. 2022.
2. Charles S. Gascon and Jacob Haas. "The Impact of COVID-19 on the Residential Real Estate Market." *Federal Reserve Bank of St. Louis*, 6 Oct. 2020, stlouisfed.org. Accessed 31 Mar. 2022.
3. Adedayo Akala. "Why America Is Moving." *NPR*, 14 Mar. 2021, npr.org. Accessed 31 Mar. 2022.
4. Nathaniel Lee. "Here's Why Experts Believe the US Is in a Housing Boom." *CNBC*, 2 Sept. 2021, cnbc.com. Accessed 31 Mar. 2022.
5. Kelli Kennedy. "COVID-19 Pet Boom." *Associated Press*, 12 May 2021, apnews.com. Accessed 31 Mar. 2022.
6. Kenneth T. Rosen et al. "Housing Is Critical Infrastructure." *Rosen Consulting Group*, June 2021, cdn.nar.realtor. Accessed 31 Mar. 2022.
7. Lee, "Here's Why Experts Believe the US Is in a Housing Boom."
8. Don Magruder. "Around the House: Housing Starts to Plummet." *Daily Commercial*, 13 June 2020, dailycommercial.com. Accessed 31 Mar. 2022.
9. Jeff Ostrowski. "High Lumber Prices Are Easing." *Pittsburgh Post-Gazett*e, 25 June 2021, post-gazette.com. Accessed 31 Mar. 2022.
10. Kristian Hernández. "Twice as Many US Renters Fell Behind on Payments during the Pandemic." *Pew*, 7 July 2021, pewtrusts.org. Accessed 31 Mar. 2022.
11. Clifford Colby and Dale Smith. "The Federal Eviction Moratorium Is Gone." *CNET*, 3 Sept. 2021, cnet.com. Accessed 31 Mar. 2022.

CHAPTER 9. HEALTH-CARE BILLS

1. John D. Birkmeyer et al. "The Impact of the COVID-19 Pandemic on Hospital Admissions in the United States." *Health Affairs*, 24 Sept. 2020, healthaffairs.org. Accessed 31 Mar. 2022.
2. David M. Cutler. "How COVID-19 Changes the Economics of Health Care." *JAMA Network*, 2 Sept. 2021, jamanetwork.com. Accessed 31 Mar. 2022.
3. "COVID-19 Impact Assessment Survey—The First Year." *American Nurses Association*, n.d., nursingworld.org. Accessed 31 Mar. 2022.
4. Cutler, "How COVID-19 Changes the Economics of Health Care."
5. "Ten Ways Coronavirus Has Changed the World Economy." *Economic Times*, 30 Dec. 2020, economictimes.indiatimes.com. Accessed 31 Mar. 2022.
6. Amy Ta. "Inflation Is High Due to COVID, Fed Policy, Supply Chain Issues." *KCRW*, 10 Nov. 2021, kcrw.com. Accessed 31 Mar. 2022.
7. "Fed Chief: Pandemic Has Permanently Changed Economy." *Boston Herald*, 17 Aug. 2021, bostonherald.com. Accessed 31 Mar. 2022.
8. "Fed Chief: Pandemic Has Permanently Changed Economy."

109

INDEX

airlines, 12, 41, 44
Amazon, 52, 54, 62
artificial intelligence (AI), 97

Black Death, 28

Centers for Disease Control and Prevention, US (CDC), 42, 88
China, 58, 64
  Wuhan, China, 17
computer chips, 64–65
Congress, US, 7, 8, 33, 50, 88
Consumer Confidence Index, 24, 25
Coronavirus Aid, Relief, and Economic Security (CARES) Act, 9–10, 12, 14, 22, 34, 88
cruise industry, 42–45

deaths, 12, 28, 94
Department of Labor, US, 5–7, 18, 19
digital nomads, 36
dollar stores, 66
DoorDash, 72

education, 27, 31, 36–37, 42, 99

essential businesses, 21, 32
Etsy, 58

Families First Coronavirus Response Act, 33
Federal Reserve Board, US, 6, 50, 99
fitness, 34, 40

gaming, 53–54, 64
gig workers, 10–11, 34
Google, 56
Great Recession, 7, 9, 84
grocery stores, 21, 32, 61, 73–77, 78
gross domestic product (GDP), 7, 9, 13, 17, 18, 25, 58, 71
Grubhub, 72
gyms, 21, 39, 40

hand sanitizer, 59, 61–62, 76
health care, 10, 21, 33, 57, 87, 93, 95
hazardous waste, 95
health-care workers, 34, 92–93, 94
hospitals, 59, 91, 94
nursing homes, 91

hotels, 21, 30, 31, 35, 39, 41, 44–45, 52, 87
housing, 17, 81–82, 84–85, 87
  construction, 85–86
  evictions, 82, 88–89
  homelessness, 87
  lumber, 85–86
  mortgages, 82, 84, 89
  rent, 81–82, 84, 87–89
  sales, 82
  vacancies, 87

inflation, 6, 44, 96
Instacart, 51
Instagram, 41

JBS pork plant, 75
JCPenney, 52
just-in-time (JIT) manufacturing, 63

low-wage jobs, 27, 30, 31, 34–35, 98

manufacturing, 21, 23, 56, 59, 62–63, 65
McConnell, Mitch, 7
McLean, Malcolm, 69
meal kits, 78
Mehta, Apoorva, 51

110

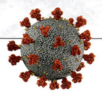

Microsoft, 53, 55
Moderna, 58

National Basketball Association (NBA), 52
National Bureau of Economic Research (NBER), 7, 13
Nintendo, 53

Orchard Point Oyster Co., 74

Pandemic Unemployment Assistance (PUA), 34
panic buying, 61
Pelosi, Nancy, 9
people of color, 27–28, 33–34, 87, 98
pets, 83
Pfizer, 59
Port of Savannah, 68–69
Powell, Jerome, 6, 99

restaurants, 19, 30, 35, 39, 41–42, 57, 71–75, 78

retail, 7, 21, 24, 45–46, 50, 52, 56–57, 61, 66, 75–76, 83, 95

services, 6–7, 13, 18, 25, 28, 30, 31, 39–40, 45–46, 49, 57, 63–64, 71, 74–75, 88, 93, 96
businesses, 21, 39, 45
delivery, 39, 49, 51, 57, 66, 71–73, 75, 77, 78, 79
jobs, 36
subscription services, 41, 53–54
shipping, 63, 66–69
small businesses, 5, 11, 12, 22, 45–46
social distancing, 40, 72–73, 77
stimulus packages, 9
stimulus payments, 40, 47, 96
stock markets, 5, 18, 20, 22, 49
Dow Jones Industrial Average, 17–20, 49
S&P 500, 5, 17, 50

supply chains, 62, 64–65, 66, 73, 96, 97

Twitch, 41, 53

unemployment, 5–6, 9–10, 12, 14, 18, 19, 23, 27–28, 29, 31, 34–35

vaccines, 8, 10, 15, 35, 58–59, 97

wages, 27, 28, 30, 31, 33–36, 66, 98
Washington, DC, 21
women, 27–28, 33, 98
work hours, 21, 23, 29, 63, 69, 72, 92
working from home, 14–15, 21, 27, 32, 36–37, 54, 56, 61–62, 95
World Health Organization (WHO), 19
World War II, 13

Zoom, 54–55

111

ABOUT THE AUTHOR

JILL C. WHEELER

Jill C. Wheeler is the author of more than 300 nonfiction titles for young readers. Her interests include biographies, along with natural and behavioral sciences. She lives in Minneapolis, Minnesota, where she enjoys asking questions, reading, sailing, and riding motorcycles.

ABOUT THE CONSULTANT

TYLER C. SCHIPPER

Tyler C. Schipper is an associate professor in the Department of Economics at the University of St. Thomas. His research focuses on real-time forecasting and issues related to informality in developing countries. He regularly appears on local media to explain economic topics and what they mean to real people. He lives in Minneapolis, Minnesota, with his wife and two children.